Teresa Severini Zaganelli

GRAPES IN THE GLASS

WINE: KNOW-HOW, FUN AND RESPONSIBILITY

GRIBAUDO

I wish to thank everyone who supported my idea, particularly Luciano and his patience, Valeria and her precision, Grazia and her enthusiasm.

GRAPES IN THE GLASS
Wine: know-how, fun and responsibility

Illustrations: Luciano Carrera
Graphic design: Le Fucine Art&Media
English translation: Valeria Cazzola

Redazione Edizioni Gribaudo
Via Garofoli, 262 - San Giovanni Lupatoto (VR)
tel. 045 6152479 fax 045 615244
e-mail: redazione@gribaudo.it

Editorial responsible: Franco Busti
Editor in chief: Laura Rapelli
Editor: Sara Sorio
Graphics responsible: Monica Priante
Photolithography and prepress: Federico Cavallon, Fabio Compri
Editorial secretary: Daniela Albertini

Printed by Grafiche Busti srl - Colognola ai Colli (VR)

© **Edizioni Gribaudo srl**
Via Natale Battaglia, 12 - 20127 Milano

First edition: 2011 [2(Ae)] 978-88-580-0364-0

Want to become a winemaking apprentice?
Then join us, jump in the bus and experience a special
day in the vineyards, winery and many things to discover.
You will be one of the students visiting and I'm sure that,
whatever your age, you will follow us... with gusto!

Today in science class, the teacher talked about how grapes - those delicious bunches, the fruits of the vine - are transformed into wine thanks to wonderful Mother Nature and the work of man. At the teacher's words, Francesco's thoughts go to his mum, who actually makes wine, since her job is related to a vineyard and winery. That's right, his mum is an **enologist**, and she will certainly be happy to show the class how **vines** are cultivated and how to make good wine, better yet, excellent wine! Francesco was not mistaken. As soon as he mentioned it to his mum, his enthusiasm rubbed off: his friends and teacher are all invited to visit the vineyards and winery in Torgiano! What's more, it's September and that means harvest: no better time to visit!

So Francesco, his friends and teacher board the bus and embark on their special journey, like true **wine tourists**.

The meeting point is right in the **vineyard**, where the harvest is already underway.

FROM PREHISTORIC TIMES

WE MUST GO VERY FAR BACK IN TIME TO TELL THE LONG STORY OF WINE. EVEN FURTHER BACK THAN WHAT YOU ARE THINKING RIGHT NOW.

IT WOULD APPEAR, IN FACT, THAT *VITIS VINIFERA* - THE SPECIES THAT ALMOST ALL FRUIT-BEARING VINES NOW BELONG TO - HAS LIVED ON OUR PLANET SINCE PREHISTORIC TIMES AND THAT INDEED IT WAS ONE OF THE FIRST PLANTS TO GROW SPONTANEOUSLY 50 MILLION YEARS AGO: AT THAT TIME, IT WAS ACTUALLY *VITIS SILVESTRIS*, WHICH LATER BECAME ACCLIMATIZED.

WINE ROADS:
ITINERARIES THAT CONNECT WINERIES, WINESHOPS AND POINTS OF INTEREST DEDICATED TO THE CULTURE AND HISTORY OF WINE, SUCH AS THE FAMOUS WINE MUSEUM OF THE LUNGAROTTI FOUNDATION LOCATED IN TORGIANO ALONG THE STRADA DEI VINI DEL CANTICO (CANTICLE WINE ROAD)

TORGIANO
CITTÀ DEL VINO

ENOLOGIST (or winemaker): a professional who oversees the entire process of transforming grapes into wine. The term derives from Greek: *oinos* (wine) and *logos* (study, science).

VINE (botanical name *Vitis*): a genus of plants from the *Vitaceae* family. Among the existing species, deriving from prehistoric *Vitis silvestris*, the most important is *Vitis vinifera* to which almost all and, therefore, the wine-producing varieties, belong. It is a climbing plant, whose branches are called vine-shoots that also sprout thin spiralling offshoots, or tendrils. The fruit of the vine is the grape.

VINEYARD: a field planted exclusively with vines. In the past, a specialized vineyard was inconceivable. Cultivation was mixed, or "promiscuous": vines were planted alongside (or "married to", as they used to say) the trunks of other plants, on which they would climb, called "tutor trees", such as olive, mulberry or poplar trees. They were planted in rows along tracts of land cultivated with crops such as wheat. This was so because the farmer needed to grow the greatest possible variety of crops to support his family. Today wine-growing is a specialized cultivation, with only vines planted in rows at a set distance both between each other and along each row. The number of vines and the layout of rows can vary due to soil characteristics and conformation: on an average, there are 4,000 to 5,000 vines (plants) per hectare (to better imagine it: 1 hectare, abbreviated ha., equals 10,000 square metres... just under one and a half soccer fields).

WINE TOURIST: a tourist who loves to search for wine in the territory where it originates and flourishes. Wine tourists travel along organized itineraries, the so-called Wine Roads.

It's fall, the most beautiful time of the year, here in Torgiano, on the rolling hills of Umbria, central Italy. The **harvest** is the season when a whole year's work in the vineyard is rewarded with many bunches of **grapes** loaded with juice that will soon become wine.

Francesco's mum arranges everyone in a circle, inviting their teacher by her side and begins explaining how to obtain tasty and healthy grapes at the end of a long cycle in which nature and man work together. You need a lot of patience and above all, great respect for the land and the environment. If the earth is well taken care of, it will continue to nourish the vines year after year and the vine-grower will be able to guide its growth and make it produce the best fruit.

In the vineyard there are many women and men harvesting: pruning shears in hand, they carefully pick the ripe bunches.

Not far away, in another vineyard, a harvesting machine is operating. It is very tall and almost looks like a space shuttle! Harvesting grapes by machine is faster than by hand, but the atmosphere is certainly a lot less fun!

FROM PREHISTORIC TIMES

IT APPEARS THAT WINE PRODUCTION BEGAN "ONLY" 7,000 YEARS AGO, ACCORDING TO ARCHEOLOGICAL FINDS; SOME SPECIALISTS CLAIM THAT WINE WAS PRODUCED FOR THE FIRST TIME, PERHAPS BY ACCIDENT, BETWEEN 9,000 AND 10,000 YEARS AGO IN THE TRANSCAUCASIAN REGION THAT NOW CORRESPONDS TO ARMENIA AND GEORGIA. IT IS CERTAIN, HOWEVER, THAT LARGE-SCALE PRODUCTION OF WINE BEGAN JUST AFTER 3000 B.C., THAT IS, ABOUT 5,000 YEARS AGO.

GRAPE: the fruit of the vine. It has the form of a cluster, consisting of a grape-stalk branching out into various racemules to which the grapes (technically, berries) are attached, either light in colour (golden yellow or green) in the case of white grapes, or dark (pink, violet or black) in the case of red grapes. Berries are composed of skin, pulp and grape-pips, or seeds – generally two – that together with the skin are a vital source of tannins (page 13) and therefore of resveratrol, a very important component for human health (page 27). The grape-skin is protected by a waxy substance (bloom) that during ripening prevents it from losing water by evaporation and defends it from attacks by micro-organisms. The fermentation of grapes produces wine, while the distillation of grapes results in *Grappa* (Italian) and *Marc* (French) and the distillation of wine – and not grapes! – produces Brandy, Armagnac and Cognac.

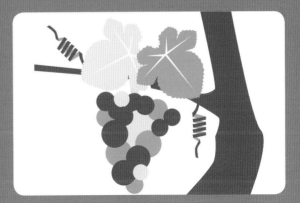

GRAPE HARVEST: picking of the grapes. It occurs between August and October, in the northern hemisphere, as the grapes ripen and reach a balance between sugar and acidity. Generally speaking, white grapes ripen before red ones.
Harvesting can be both manual and mechanical:
- manual: the harvester cuts each bunch at the base with large scissors called pruning shears;
- mechanical: a large harvesting machine straddles the vineyard rows to collect grapes by detaching them from the stalk.

"Before talking about harvesting and vinification" continues Francesco's mum, "you must be aware that vines have to be cared for continuously. Appropriate vineyard operations are helpful for moderating vine development and favour good nourishment for the fruit. In winter, when the vine is bare, it is pruned to remove the shoots (**branchlets**) that produced fruit the previous year and have become old; then it must be *fertilized* (cow manure is perfect!) to nourish it. In spring the vine vegetates and then blooms, but at the beginning of summer, excess vegetation must be thinned out – "green pruning" – so the vine will put all its strength into forming and nourishing the grapes. In July it's necessary to thin out the **vine leaves** that cover the bunches, so the sun can easily reach them. Finally, in August, some of those bunches are eliminated so the remaining ones will ripen better. Throughout the year, the soil is periodically hoed to keep the vines free from weeds that could "rob" water and nourishment from the vine and... a watch is kept on the birds so they don't eat the grapes as they ripen.

Not all grape varieties grow at the same rate. There are **varietals**, called precocious (early ripening), that have different requirements from the late-ripening ones that bud and ripen later.

As we'll see later on, knowledge and experience are needed, but...

TIP

Try collecting leaves from various varietals, press them under a weight and let them dry between two sheets of newspaper and mount on pieces of paper. Write the name of the varietal beside each one and note their distinctive characters. You can start a specialized herbarium that could even become a record-breaking collection!

A BIT OF HISTORY

THE FIRST EVIDENCE OF VITICULTURE AND VINIFICATION GOES BACK TO THE ANCIENT EGYPTIANS: BECAUSE ONLY RED GRAPES, TYPICAL OF TEMPERATE CLIMATES, ARE DEPICTED ON THE FRESCOES OF THEIR TOMBS, WE SUPPOSE THAT THEIR WINES WERE GENERALLY RED. WITH THE EMERGENCE OF OTHER CIVILIZATIONS, THE VARIOUS CONQUERING PEOPLES SPREAD THE VINE FURTHER NORTH ALONG THE MEDITERRANEAN COAST. EARLIER THAN 2,000 B.C., THE PHOENICIANS HAD BROUGHT NEW VARIETIES OF *VITIS VINIFERA SATIVA* AND NEW CULTIVATION TECHNIQUES TO SICILY. ITALY WAS EVEN CALLED "ENOTRIA", THE LAND OF THE VINE, AND SOPHOCLES (5TH CENTURY B.C.) PROCLAIMED IT "THE LAND FAVOURED BY BACCHUS".

BRANCHLETS: the shoots or twigs that are eliminated during pruning. They are residues that until recently were considered useless and needed to be removed from the field and burned because they could breed micro-organisms causing vine diseases. Now, thanks to scientific research, this waste matter can be used to produce "renewable" energy by burning them in special "biomass" furnaces: this energy is then transformed into heat and steam and even into refrigeration. This way, the vine completes a full cycle, contributes to safeguarding our planet and can give us the satisfaction of drinking a wine produced only with energy from reusing by-products of the vine!

VARIETAL: term that indicates a specific variety of grape, such as Sangiovese, Merlot, etc. Varietals are distinguished by the shape and colour of the bunch and leaves, by ripening times and, above all, by the different characteristics of wines obtained from them. In terms of the place where they are grown, they are defined as native, if cultivated in a certain area since time immemorial, to distinguish them from varietals imported from other areas. A wine can be produced with a blend of grapes of different varietals or can be a single vine variety, if it comes from just one varietal (for example Sagrantino di Montefalco wine, which is made from 100% Sagrantino grapes). It is estimated that about 5,000 grape varietals are cultivated world-wide.

VINE LEAF: is heart-shaped with 5 indented lobes with a serrated edge. Each variety has different indentations: ampelography is the study of the correspondence between grape variety and leaf shape. In fall – depending on the varietal – the leaves take on an intense golden or red colour, after which they gradually fall and the vine remains bare.

... the work of the vine grower, however specialized he may be, is not enough! We must take into consideration climate variability (hail, frost, too much or too little rain, excessive heat) although now technology can come to the rescue in critical conditions. Nonetheless, if the season goes badly, all that hard work could be lost!" Just as we mention this, the students notice a small robot situated at the edge of the vineyard. It is a special **meteorological station** that monitors the climatic conditions in the vineyard and therefore facilitates the work of Attilio, the **agronomist**. Just as his name is men-

tioned, he arrives to check the ripening of the grapes and is pleased to respond to the questions arising from the curious students.

"The ideal climate for ripening grapes is a dry one with temperatures that are not excessively high" stresses Attilio. "In addition, especially during the harvest, it is particularly useful to have a good **temperature range** between day and night and a light wind – not too strong! – to keep the bunches dry. Fortunately, during these harvesting days, the sky is blue and there is no risk of rain. The temperature is hot during the day and cool at night, without excesses, and the wind is just a breeze – the ideal conditions for a good harvest!"

AGRONOMIST: an expert in agriculture. In our case, a specialist in "viticulture" who supervises vine cultivation. His work in the vineyard precedes that of the enologist in the winery, and is a fundamental link in the entire chain of specialists that work to produce a good wine.

METEOROLOGICAL STATION: a machine that detects the amount of precipitation, air temperature and humidity. The more technologically advanced stations collect data by computer and elaborate them, indicating in real time when it is time to intervene and combat – or possibly prevent – vine diseases caused by unfavourable weather.

TEMPERATURE RANGE: the variation in temperature between day and night. It promotes grape maturation and increases sugar content. It also increases the colour intensity of the resulting wine, conferring greater body and more decisive aroma.

A happy chorus thanks and says goodbye to Attilio, who goes back to his work.

"We have seen the ideal conditions for grape ripening and now" says Francesco's mum, "let's continue with the elements found in the grape and see how they change as it ripens. The message is a simple one:

NATURE IS TRULY A FASCINATING LABORATORY!!

Let's just think, for example, about the richness of possible combinations, since each varietal transmits specific characteristics to wine: intensity of colour, scents and flavour. The diversity is also enhanced by soil quality, exposure to sun and winds and, more generally, by climate. Other influences stem from the way the vine is cultivated.

Grapes = wine: seems easy right? In reality, it's a bit more complicated than that...

To better understand it, let's go back to our ripe grapes. The elements that give colour, aroma and consistency to the wine are numerous: shall we name a few? They have complicated names, but in time they will become familiar to us: **polyphenols**, – and among these, **tannins** and **anthocyanins** – along with **vitamins**, **mineral substances**, **odourous substances**, **sugars** and other microelements.

It may seem incredible, but there is also water, and lots of it: between 75 and 80%!

The components will be more concentrated in the grapes depending on how much "mother vine" is able to nourish them, and also helps us understand why a good farmer thins out the bunches in August, leaving only a limited number to ripen in the best way.

A BIT OF HISTORY

THE WINE OF OUR ANCESTORS WAS QUITE DIFFERENT FROM WINE NOWADAYS: TO PRESERVE IT AND PROBABLY TO COVER POSSIBLE DEFECTS, THEY USED TO ADD SPICES, HONEY, MACERATED HERBS, OR SEA-WATER. IT WAS HIGH IN ALCOHOL BECAUSE THE GRAPES WOULD BE PICKED WHEN OVERRIPE. KEPT IN WARM CONDITIONS, AND THEREFORE SYRUPY IN CONSISTENCY, THE WINE OF THE ANCIENT ROMANS NEEDED TO BE DILUTED WITH WATER – GENERALLY 3 PARTS TO 5 – BY POURING FIRST THE WATER AND THEN THE WINE, AS XENOPHON (4TH CENT. B.C.) TELLS US: "IF YOU POUR YOURSELF A DRINK, NEVER PUT THE WINE IN YOUR GLASS OR CUP FIRST, BUT FIRST THE WATER AND THEN THE WINE ON TOP". DRINKING UNDILUTED WINE WAS EVEN CONSIDERED BARBARIC!

ANTHOCYANINS: colouring substances present in the skins of red grapes that are passed on to the wine. The colour intensity of a red or rosé wine doesn't only depend on the degree of ripening of the grapes, but also on the duration of contact between skins and juice during fermentation. The longer the contact, the more anthocyanins pass into the wine, the more intense the colour of the wine.

MINERAL SUBSTANCES: those contained in wine are: potassium, manganese, iron, calcium, magnesium, phosphorus, iodine, arsenic, carbon, boron.

ODOROUS SUBSTANCES: these are compounds (terpenes) that determine the intensity of a wine's aroma. There are many different types, among which is geraniol, so called because it can also be smelled in geranium plants. In some grapes, called aromatic varietals, such as Traminer, the aromas remain unaltered during fermentation, giving the wine particularly fragrant and fruity scents.

POLYPHENOLS: components of wine found in the skins and stems of grapes that are responsible for colour and flavour: they are formed as the grape ripens during summer, thanks to sun exposure. Polyphenols are important for our health because they are powerful antioxidants and help to lower blood cholesterol. They have anti-inflammatory and tumour-preventing properties. Compared to white wine, reds have a higher level of phenolic compounds because during fermentation the juice remains in contact with skins and pips.

SUGARS: substances responsible for the sweetness of foods. Those present in grapes are laevulose, fructose, glucose and dextrose.

TANNINS: substances found in red grapes – as well as in many other fruits – and in wine. They are responsible for the sensation of astringency that you perceive when drinking a very young red wine, like when you taste fruit that is not yet ripe.

It's easy to imagine that, since there are so many different types of varietals, the combinations of wines that can be produced are endless.

The first distinction to be made, however, is between **table grapes** – for eating, with or without seeds (pips) – and **wine grapes**, that are suitable for vinification. In general, wine cannot be produced with table grapes. Wine grapes, on the other hand, can be eaten like the others and are, in fact, very tasty.

"These in front of us, hanging from the vines and ready to be picked, are wine grapes and they certainly look inviting! And as we examine them closely, so full and ripe, everything that we have listened to earlier prepares us to go to the heart of the subject of "wine" with a desire to know more about it".

"And now, a great idea to get everyone involved! Each member of the group will carefully pick a bunch of grapes, personally bring it to the winery and add it to the others in the same **vat** or tub (not the tub used for taking a bath, though!), where all the bunches are unloaded from the tractors." Back at home, the students can proudly report on how they contributed to the good wine Torgiano Rosso DOC of this year.

Francesco has already done this many other times and since he knows perfectly well that when picking from the vine one must choose only the good, ripe bunches, leaving behind the damaged ones, he helps his friends pick the best clusters.

A BIT OF HISTORY

AMONG THE ANCIENT ROMANS, WINE COULD BE DRUNK ONLY BY MEN: IT WAS PROHIBITED TO ROMAN MATRONS AND A HUSBAND COULD EVEN RENOUNCE HIS WIFE IF HE MERELY SUSPECTED THAT SHE HAD DRUNK WINE. IT'S EASY TO IMAGINE, THEN, THAT THE CUSTOM OF SALUTING WITH A KISS ORIGINATES FROM THE NEED TO VERIFY IF A WOMAN SMELLED OF *TEMETUM* (THE ANCIENT NAME FOR WINE). THERE CERTAINLY COULD NOT HAVE BEEN WOMEN ENOLOGISTS AT THAT TIME!

TABLE GRAPES: the grapes normally destined for food use that generally have large berries. Some of the main white varieties are: Italia, Vittoria and Regina while the reds are Red Globe and Rosada. They can be consumed either fresh or dried (raisins). Specific varieties are used for raisins: Sultana, Black Corinth, Malaga or those from Smyrna, which are all apyretic (seedless) and high in sugar. Grapes contain – among other substances – Omega-3, which is a rich antioxidant. They have many healthful properties and should be eaten whole, with skins (rich in vitamins A and K) and seeds (containing acids that help prevent some tumour-causing diseases).

VAT: a large container for wine. It can be closed or open. The vat mentioned in the text is an open one into which the grapes are transferred upon arriving at the winery. The vats where the fermentation takes place are cylindrical and closed. Later, the wine is kept in closed vats before being transferred to wooden casks or directly to the bottle. Nowadays, these containers are generally in stainless steel (that doesn't interact with the wine), but vats in cement (internally vitrified to guarantee hygienic conditions), as well as in glass resin or wood, are still used.

WINE GRAPES: suitable for vinification, they have small and compact berries. There are hundreds of varieties, each one having particular characteristics that appear in the wine that they produce.

The students are joyful and excited about everything they have attentively listened to and observed: "What they are learning today could be part of their work tomorrow," says Francesco's mum, "and so it's important that they are familiar with the basics of this fascinating enological world". Also, at the end of the trip, the teacher could ask them to prepare a report on what they've seen and learned... that's right, better not get distracted!

In the past, the traditions that fathers used to pass on to their sons regulated the series of tasks to do in the countryside. The rhythm of agricultural work was at one with life in general, each crop had its own season and was part of the cycle of nature. Nowadays working outdoors, in touch with nature and the environment, occupies increasingly smaller numbers of people, perhaps because working in factories and offices seems more comfortable, but can we be sure? Visiting vineyards and wineries, reading stories like this one, can also help preserve the memory of a different style of life and recognize how living conditions now are more comfortable than those of the past and, so, how attractive this profession immersed in nature can be.

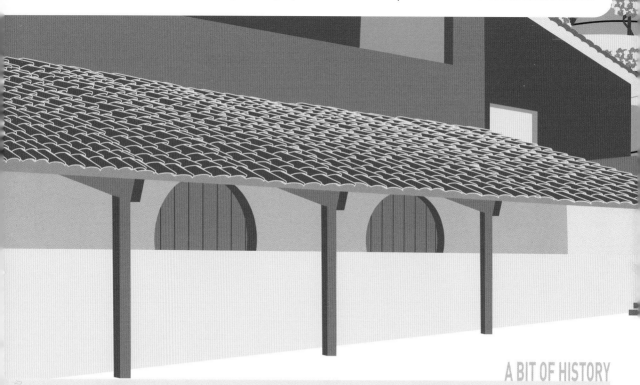

A BIT OF HISTORY

IN ANCIENT GREECE, THE KNOWLEDGE OF HOW TO PRODUCE QUALITY WINE WAS A SIGN OF CIVILIZATION: "THE MAN WHO USES WINE IS CIVILIZED, THE ONE WHO DOESN'T IS A BARBARIAN", THE GREEK WOULD SAY. AND THE SO-CALLED "BARBARIANS" PRINCIPALLY CONSUMED BEER. THE MEAL HAD AN ALMOST RELIGIOUS CHARACTER: AN INVISIBLE GOD WOULD PRESIDE OVER IT AND, IN HIS HONOUR, THE MASTER OF THE HOUSE WOULD SPRINKLE A FEW DROPS OF WINE FROM A SPECIAL CUP ONTO THE FLOOR OR IN THE FIREPLACE, AT THE BEGINNING AND END OF EACH MEAL.

In the past, harvest in the countryside was organized like a real celebration: simple, but very heartfelt, a sort of rite that used to conclude the major agricultural crops, helping to forget about the hardship of the many days of labour and as a good omen to lighten the preoccupation for a good harvest.

Celebrations used to be held:
– in July, for the reaping of wheat;
– in August, for the stripping of the corn harvest;
– in September, for the stringing of tobacco;
– in October, for the grape harvest. This was probably the most anticipated of all and involved everyone at the farm with great festiveness, also because the fruit of the harvest was immediately and tangibly transformed into wine. After the grapes had been picked, brought to the cellars and unloaded into open concrete or brick vats, accordion music used to accompany the pressing: there would be dancing to merry jumping refrains and stomping on the grapes while juice flowed from the spout into fermentation vats or casks – a grand celebration in which great fun was had by all! Even many engagements came about as a result, since in order to avoid prolonging the operations, on such occasions the families of several farmers would gather and work together.

Nowadays, many of these celebrations no longer take place and almost all the work is mechanized: it is certainly less tiring and, as in the case of the harvest, the final product is of better quality, but it is truly a shame that such deeply felt traditions have completely disappeared, and certain others have even been forgotten! For Saint Martin's day on November 11th, it was customary – and still now this tradition is alive in the countryside – to drink the new wine. This custom was so important and valued that it has inspired many poems, such as the one dedicated to San Martino on the next page. In the past, schoolchildren used to learn these lovely poems by heart and this also aided in passing down traditions.

It is useful to know that conventionally San Martino marks the beginning of the agricultural year.

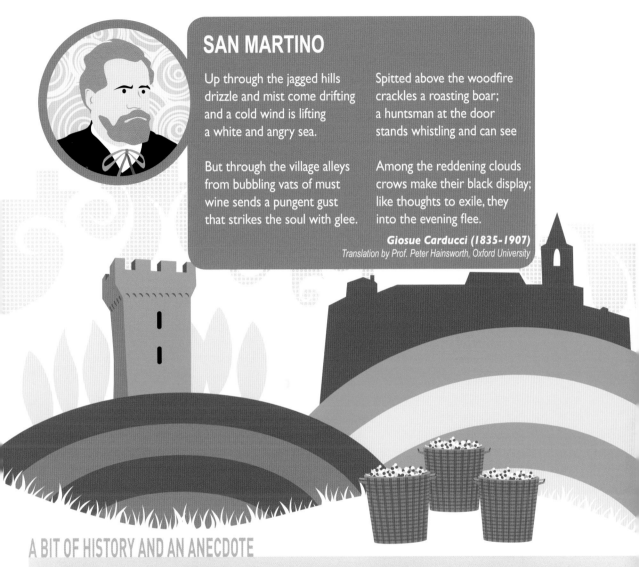

SAN MARTINO

Up through the jagged hills
drizzle and mist come drifting
and a cold wind is lifting
a white and angry sea.

But through the village alleys
from bubbling vats of must
wine sends a pungent gust
that strikes the soul with glee.

Spitted above the woodfire
crackles a roasting boar;
a huntsman at the door
stands whistling and can see

Among the reddening clouds
crows make their black display;
like thoughts to exile, they
into the evening flee.

Giosue Carducci (1835-1907)
Translation by Prof. Peter Hainsworth, Oxford University

A BIT OF HISTORY AND AN ANECDOTE

IN ANTIQUITY, WINE USED TO BE STORED AND TRANSPORTED IN TERRACOTTA AMPHORAS WITH A POINTED BOT-
TOM. THIS PARTICULAR SHAPE WAS VERY USEFUL DURING MARITIME TRANSPORT: IN THE HOLDS OF SHIPS, THESE
VASES WOULD BE BURIED UPRIGHT IN ROWS IN A LAYER OF SAND SPREAD ON THE FLOOR. THE ROWS ABOVE WOULD
BE FITTED IN WITHIN THE EMPTY SPACES OF THE LOWER ROW AND THE ENSEMBLE REMAINED "FLEXIBLE" ENOUGH
TO BE TRANSPORTED WITHOUT RISKING BREAKAGE EVEN DURING STORMS. THE AMPHORAS WERE HERMETICALLY
SEALED WITH CAPS OF TERRACOTTA, WAX OR CORK SEALED WITH TAR; THE WINE WAS THEREFORE PRESERVED.
FROM THE AMPHORAS, THE WINE WAS POURED INTO LARGE BOWLS AND FROM THERE, SERVED IN CUPS. EACH AM-
PHORA CONTAINED 38 LITRES AND INSTEAD OF THE PRODUCTION YEAR, BORE A SORT OF LABEL (*PITTACIUM*) WITH
THE NAME OF THE CONSUL WHO WAS GOVERNING AT THE TIME IN THE PROVINCE WHERE THE WINE WAS PRODUCED.

Approaching the cellar, Francesco and his friends excitedly throw their bunches into the vat together with the others. The grapes release an intense bouquet. "And they are super-sweet!" says Francesco, who, along with his friends, has tasted a few berries. And he's absolutely right, because ripe grapes are sweet and tasty. The sweetness is due to the sugar content of the berries: the more sugar, the sweeter the must and, above all, the higher the alcohol content of the wine that will be produced at the end of **fermentation**, when the sugar will be transformed, like magic, into **ethyl alcohol** and **carbon dioxide**.

At these words the teacher reminds the students of a lesson held at school, mentioning that **Louis Pasteur**, the great French biologist, was the first to demonstrate that fermentation is produced by the activity of **yeasts**. With his numerous studies on wine, he paved the way for the technological development of enology. He defined wine as *the most hygienic of beverages,* even more so than water, that, on the contrary, can often be polluted!

For all these reasons, before each harvest, the agronomist takes samples on various dates of random grape clusters in the different vineyards, bringing them to the enologist, who measures the **sugar content**. Together they decide when to begin the harvest: the work of the agronomist must therefore be synchronized with that of the enologist! It would be a great mistake to pick the grapes too early or too late.

LOUIS PASTEUR
The French scientist considered the founder of modern microbiology. On order of Emperor Napoleon III, he conducted the first scientific studies on wine and illustrated them in the book *Études sur le vin* (Studies on wine) whose first edition was published in 1866.

CARBON DIOXIDE: indicated by the chemical formula CO_2, it is a volatile substance that is formed by the fermentation of must together with ethyl alcohol. It dissipates into the air as soon as it is formed by the association of oxygen and carbon. On the basis of the CO_2 content, wines can be distinguished as either "sparkling" or "still": the bubbles that in sparkling wines incessantly move up to the surface when the bottle is opened and the wine is poured into the glass are in fact bubbles of CO_2.

ETHYL ALCOHOL: produced by yeast during the transformation of grapes. The more ethyl alcohol in a wine, the greater the sensation of "robustness". The alcohol content of a wine must appear on the wine label. Therefore, if we find 12.5% alcohol, we know that in the given wine, out of 100 ml, 12.5 of them are of ethyl alcohol. Coincidentally, the word alcohol derives from the Arab *al-khol* ("essence").

FERMENTATION: the process by which the sugars present in the must are transformed into ethyl alcohol and carbon dioxide, with a release of heat.

SUGAR CONTENT: the amount of sugar in the must. It is measured in "Babo degrees", a unit of measurement that corresponds to 1 gram of sugar in 100 grams of must. From 1 gram of sugar, about 0.6 ml of alcohol is obtained. Therefore, a grape containing 20% of sugar (or 20 Babo degrees) gives a 12% alcohol content in the wine.

YEASTS: single-celled micro-organisms, so small that they are not visible to the naked eye. They are found naturally in the grape or can be "sown" or added to the grape juice to improve fermentation. They belong to the *Saccaromyces* family and the most common is *Saccaromyces Cerevisiae*, also responsible for making bread dough rise.

And now... READY... SET... GO! This is the adventure that will introduce us to the secrets of enology. All together, we will follow the journey of those beautiful clusters of red grapes of Sangiovese and Canaiolo varieties, and see the specific operations for obtaining a good red wine. "And," as Francesco's mum points out again, "it's truly a fascinating adventure involving biology, chemistry and physics, where the work of men and women has an important role in obtaining a wine with particular characteristics, elegant and flavourful. Starting with colour, which is not accidental: while wines can be **white**, **red** or **rosé**, the **vinification** techniques to produce these colours are different from one another and don't depend solely on grape colour.

VINIFICATION

RED VINIFICATION: the process described in the story; it calls for a period of maceration of liquid on the marc (see page 29) even after fermentation.

WHITE VINIFICATION: the transformation process for obtaining white wine, starting with either white or red grapes and separating the skins from the juice as soon as possible. Enological techniques can influence colour intensity, from very light to golden yellow. In general, white vinification includes the following steps:

destemming to eliminate the stems;

pressing of the berries softly to prevent certain substances from passing from the skin into the juice;

refrigeration of the destemmed, crushed mass to prevent fermentation from commencing;

draining to eliminate the marc;

alcoholic fermentation with cooling of the must to transform it into wine;

wood aging (in the case of very structured wines);

decantation to separate the free-run wine from the lees;

refrigeration to stabilize the wine by encouraging the formation of tartrates, the mineral salts that must then be eliminated;

filtration to eliminate tartrates and impurities;

bottling.

ROSÉ VINIFICATION: an intermediate process between the two preceding ones that requires leaving the skins of the red grapes in contact with the juice for just a few hours. The resulting wine has a lovely, salmon pink colour: the longer the skin contact, the more intense the colour; naturally obtaining a red wine, if maceration is not interrupted.

Let's start with the colour: from white grapes we can produce only white wine, while red grapes can produce either red, white or rosé wines. This is because – as we have seen – the anthocyanins (page 13) that confer colour to red wine, are only found in red grape skins, while the pulp is always greenish in colour. Therefore, the contact of the red skin with the juice during **maceration** is what gives red wine its lovely red colour (hey, this sounds like a tongue-twister!).

Let's be careful, however: this maceration is not to be confused with **carbonic maceration**, a procedure that is the basis of producing Novello wine (a special type described on page 50).

Then there is temperature control, which is extremely important during both fermentation and maceration. In the case of white and rosé musts, fermentation temperature is artificially maintained lower than for red fermentation; this way it takes longer and the wine maintains the freshness and richness of scents that are typical of these two types of wine."

The story fascinates the students as they start to imagine "their" bottle of wine being produced with the bunches they harvested together...

CARBONIC MACERATION: a phase of the complex production process for Novello wine (page 50), consisting in a form of intracellular fermentation, caused not by yeasts but by enzymes – naturally present in grapes – within an environment that is saturated with carbon dioxide, CO_2. The grape bunches are put intact into a special vat with a grill that supports them before reaching bottom and air is substituted with CO_2. A small percentage of the grapes at the bottom are crushed by the weight of the others, releasing juice that trickles underneath the grill and begins to ferment thanks to the yeasts already present on the skins, producing alcohol and CO_2. This gas, together with the CO_2 initially injected into the vat, rapidly saturates the container, so the cells of the upper grapes that are not crushed, must modify their metabolism due to their enzymes and must "destroy" their own malic acid. This transformation makes the juice less acidic and softer in flavour. After 15-20 days the grapes are destemmed and pressed and the juice begins a brief phase of normal alcoholic fermentation in which the yeasts transform the residual sugar into alcohol.

MACERATION: the phase involving contact between grape-skins and juice. It continues after fermentation and is very important for transmitting the colouring substances contained in the skins to wine. To obtain a good, intense red colour, contact must last at least 6 days.

ANECDOTE

The term fermentation derives from the Latin verb fervere which means "to boil". Did you notice on page 19 how the great poet Giosue Carducci recalls "bubbling vats" in his poem "San Martino"? You can almost see and hear the wine bubbling...

...and one of the students impatiently asks when the grapes will finally become wine. "First of all" Francesco's mum continues, "we must separate the stem from the grapes to avoid the substances from the stem giving a too astringent flavour to the wine (the same flavour that we sense when eating unripe fruit). The operation of detaching the berries is called destemming and is carried out by a specific destemming machine".

"Then we must extract the juice from the grapes. This is done using a *press*, a special machine that crushes the berries, but in a "soft" way, so that the skin is not stressed and therefore doesn't harm the quality of the wine. This operation is called *pressing*, like the mechanical action that in the past farmers would apply by pressing the grapes with their feet to let the juice flow. The mixture of liquids and solids obtained is collected in special fermentation vats, for it is in these containers that the true transformation takes place – the alcoholic fermentation (page 21) during which the grape juice becomes **must** and begins to ferment, producing bubbles like boiling water does".

"Yeasts are responsible for this (yes, the very ones encountered when the teacher talked about Pasteur on page 20). These are micro-organisms that "eat" the sugar contained in the must and transform it into ethyl alcohol, carbon dioxide and the heat that causes the must to boil. It is no coincidence that this is called a 'tumultuous' fermentation: it is a process that lasts from 3 to 10 days and normally ends when the sugars have been completely transformed".

"The must – which by now has finally become wine! – progressively cools off and the marc (see page 28) is left in contact with the liquid for a few more days. In this maceration phase, a special substance originating from the pips accumulates in the wine. It is called **resveratrol**, a difficult name to remember, but a very useful substance indeed! It is what guarantees the majority of those health benefits that are generally attributed to wine".

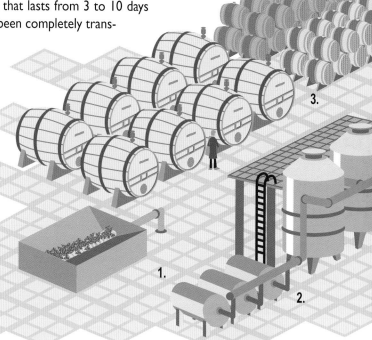

1. DESTEMMERS AND PRESSES
2. FERMENTATION, MACERATION OR STORAGE VATS
3. BARRELS AND BARRIQUES
4. BOTTLING LINE
5. BOTTLES LAID DOWN IN THE CELLAR
6. SPUMANTE BOTTLES ON PUPITRES ("SHAKING" RACKS)
7. CARTONS READY FOR SHIPMENT

MUST: the pressed juice of grapes that has begun the fermentation process. In red vinification, the must still includes skins and pips. In white and rosé vinification, the juice is separated from the solid parts more or less immediately, while the particles that still remain suspended in the must are eliminated subsequently.

RESVERATROL: a substance contained within the pips (grape seeds, page 7), that is very important for good health because it protects blood circulation in the body. For this reason, wine – and particularly red wine that has remained in contact with the pips for an extended period during fermentation and maceration – has curative properties. While excessive doses of alcohol are harmful, moderate servings of red wine (about two glasses a day) can have a positive effect on our cardiovascular system, as amply demonstrated by medical studies. Resveratrol protects from the oxidization caused by free radicals and reduces the accumulation of cholesterol in the arteries, preventing the development of arteriosclerosis and other cardiovascular diseases (it's not a coincidence that resveratrol is called "the garbage-man of the arteries"!). It also appears to have anti-inflammatory and tumor-preventing properties.

27

The journey continues and the students' attention grows. When the maceration has finished, we must separate the wine from the **marc**. We have now reached the **draining off** stage – or first decantation – under the supervision of Marco, the cellar-master. The wine is pumped from above so that the marc remains within the vat. This marc is not to be disposed of: on the contrary, it is still dripping with residual liquid that it would be a shame to waste. By crushing it in a vertical press (in the operation called pressing) we can obtain a little more wine, called press wine. This can be added to the preceding wine – which we will call "free-run" wine to distinguish it – or it can be used for a lower quality wine. The marc can also be distilled to be transformed into **grappa** or into wine alcohol – in "distilleries" and not at the winery.

DRAINING OFF: wine decantation from the vat where it has fermented to another one in order to separate the liquid from the marc.

GRAPPA: the typical Italian distilled beverage produced with marc exclusively from grapes harvested and vinified in Italy. Grappa is obtained from the marc of prized grape varieties separated after the draining off, still wet with juice. There are also grappas aromatised with herbs or fruit. Grappa is a very alcoholic beverage, so it must be consumed with great moderation! In France the term for *grappa* is *marc*. (Note the different meanings in French and English: see below).

MARC: the mixture of solid parts (seeds and skins) that is separated from the juice immediately following pressing in the case of white fermentation. In red vinification, it is after maceration.

And once again, careful with temperatures! Each one of the previous operations must occur at cool temperatures and without abrupt changes. Beware of extremes, though: particularly during fermentation, the temperature limit of the must cannot be too low, because the process wouldn't be successful, but not too high, either, otherwise the wine could have problems with "cooked" flavours. **Temperature-controlled fermentation** is the essential condition for obtaining the best results: it is guaranteed by the entire team of cellar-men guided by Marco, who works with great attention under the guidance of Vincenzo, the winery enologist (page 5). Precision is essential: even a small error could compromise the work of many other people!

Should it be necessary, there are various ways to cool down a must that tends to go above the temperature range. We can intervene from the exterior, by running cold water along the fermentation vats; or we can use internal refrigeration panels, or the latest insulated vats that work using the same principal as the insulated jugs we use for keeping beverages cool.

IN THE MIDDLE AGES, IN THE TRANQUILLITY OF THEIR MONASTERIES, MONKS EXPERIMENTED WITH NEW TECHNIQUES IN ALCHEMY, HERBALISM AND DISTILLATION, REFINING THE PROCEDURES FOR MAKING LIQUEURS AND DISTILLED DRINKS. THANKS TO THEM, MANY ANCIENT VARIETIES OF VINES WERE SAVED, DESCRIBED AND PASSED ON. ONLY AFTER THE RENAISSANCE DID THE PRODUCTION OF ITALIAN WINES BEGIN THE EXPANSION THAT OVER TIME HAS MADE THEM FAMOUS THE WORLD OVER AND HAS MADE ITALY THE PREMIER VITICULTURAL NATION IN THE WORLD. NOWADAYS, EUROPE PRODUCES 80% OF THE WORLD'S WINE.

CONTROLLED TEMPERA-TURE FERMENTATION: a practice that has been used for several decades, bringing about a great evolution in wine quality, above all in white wines. By artificially maintaining the temperature of white musts at about 16-17 °C (61-63 °F), fermentation is slowed down, preventing the volatile substances – the wine's perfume – from evaporating due to boiling. If the fermentation were left "free", the temperature would rise greatly and the process would last a short time, but quality would be inferior. In the fermentation of red musts, on the other hand, temperature can be higher. The optimal temperature range within which we can obtain quality red wines with good colour extraction and polyphenolic extraction is between 25 and 30 °C (77-86 °F).

There are some temperature limits for must: below 15 °C (59 °F) the yeasts work too slowly and the must cannot ferment. Above 38 °C (100 °F) there is a risk of a block in the fermentation and even the death of the yeasts.

So, we must be very careful that fermentation doesn't stop before it should, for example because the cellars are too cold or due other biological factors. If, for some reason, the sugar doesn't ferment completely, the wine could end up with a sweet flavour when, on the contrary, it should have been decisively "dry".

This would certainly be inconvenient. However, in some cases, this very "inconvenience" could be produced intentionally – with the use of great expertise, in order to produce a particular type of wine characterized, for example, by a basic sweetness guaranteed by a certain quantity of **residual sugars**. The possibilities are endless when we decide to produce wine, and this is the very thing that makes it so fascinating. "Even people like us, who always work with wine" adds Vincenzo, the enologist, who has joined them "never stop being surprised by the richness of sensations and the many variations that this beverage offers us!"

"Before being transformed into wine, the must is very very sweet and this is why" Francesco's mum recounts – digressing a bit to let the attentive listeners have a break – "it has always been considered a treat to drink, ever since antiquity".

"Sweet must is even used in several traditional recipes, for example to make some excellent cookies called *mostaccioli* (must cookies), typical of the harvest period all over the Umbria region. The ladies of Torgiano make excellent ones and also make bread with a similar type of dough which includes must."

A BIT OF RELIGION

THE VINE, GRAPES AND WINE HAVE OFTEN TAKEN ON SACRED MEANINGS. IN POLYTHEISTIC RELIGIONS, FOR EX-AMPLE, WINE WAS CONSIDERED A GIFT OF THE GODS: MYTHOLOGY ATTRIBUTES TO DIONYSUS - THE IMMORTAL SON OF ZEUS - THE INTRODUCTION OF VINE CULTIVATION AMONG MEN. IT IS NOT A COINCIDENCE THAT HE WAS REVERED AS THE GOD OF WINE. THE DIONYSIAN RITES ARE CONSIDERED TO HAVE ORIGINATED THEATRE, AND SO THE CENTRE OF THE ORCHESTRA IN GREEK THEATRES - WHERE THE CHOIR WOULD SING AND DANCE AND THE ACTORS PLAYED THEIR ROLES - WAS KNOWN AS THE ALTAR OF DIONYSUS ("THYMELE").

RESIDUAL SUGARS: sugars of the must that have not completely fermented and are responsible for a particular, not always noticeable sensation of "softness" (sweetness) of the wine. The higher the residual sugar, the sweeter the wine. With reference to the amount of sugar, we have wines that are:

dry, when the sugar is practically absent or imperceptible;

medium-dry, if the presence of sugar is slightly noticeable;

perceptibly sweet, if the sweet flavour is noticeable;

medium, if the presence is clearly noticeable;

medium-sweet, if the presence is clear, but not prevalent;

sweet, when the presence of sugars is prevalent.

A DELICIOUS PROJECT:
a recipe for mostaccioli - cookies with must

Just by following the recipe below, anyone can make some quite good ones. Let's try it!

INGREDIENTS FOR 6 SERVINGS:
500 gr flour (4 cups); 2 tablespoons extra virgin olive oil; 1 tablespoon sugar; fresh must of white grapes, as required; 1/2 cube of fresh yeast, or 1 package of dry yeast; 1 pinch of salt.

METHOD:
Make a mound of flo ur on the work surface or collect it in a large mixing bowl. Dissolve the yeast in warm water as per instructions, mix it with a small amount of flour. Pour the yeast mixture into the centre of the flour and cover with flour from the mound. Let rise away from drafts for 30 minutes, then mix with the oil, salt and enough must to obtain a soft, but consistent dough. Shape the dough into many finger-sized pieces about 8-10 cm/3-4 inches long, then form ring shapes by pinching the ends together. Place them on greased baking trays and bake in a 180 °C (365 °F) oven for 35-40 minutes. Let cool, then... eat them with gusto!

"Let's get back to our wine adventure then, and see how a wine can take on particular flavours and scents." "And characteristic ones!" adds Francesco, "like the one that we smell at the winery at this time of year, that invites us to be in good spirits at being part of the grape harvest!"

Francesco's mum signals to Vincenzo and invites him to show the ultramodern machines that are now used to carry out operations in the cellars and computerised quality controls. That's right! Computers are used even in the cellars to automatise and optimise operations in making wine.

And while Vincenzo speaks, the students walk along, gazing upwards at the large stainless steel cylinders that look like space towers: they are really **fermentation vats**, where the must undergoes fermentation, but an exclamation of wonder and amazement arises from the students, impressed by the spectacle.

Vincenzo reminds them that the wine will remain in those containers till after maceration, when the extraction of colour and consistency from the skins, has been completed. In order to help these processes and guarantee their best development, each day the must is **pumped-over** to break the **cap** of marc and remix the contents of the vat.

A BIT OF RELIGION

THE GREEK NAME OF THE GOD DIONYSUS BECAME BACCHUS, FROM ONE OF THE INVOCATIONS USED BY THE GOD'S FOLLOWERS (BACCHOS, BACCHIOS, BACCHUS) AND UNDER THIS NAME HE BECAME KNOWN TO THE ROMANS WHO COMPARE HIM TO LIBER, THE LATIN GOD OF FERTILITY. THIS SAME EVOLUTION OCCURRED FOR FUFLUNS, THE ETRUSCAN GOD OF PLANT LIFE WHO WAS REPLACED BY DIONYSUS.

CAP: the layer of marc that naturally rises to the top of the vats where red wines ferment, pushed up by the CO_2 that is naturally released. Since the cap is almost like a seal, it must be repeatedly broken to remix the must, agitating it to extract as much colour and flavour as possible from the solid parts of the grape and also to rapidly disperse the heat and carbon dioxide which form during fermentation.

FERMENTATION VATS: large cylindrical containers in which the must ferments. They come in various shapes and sizes and are constructed of stainless steel, cement, wood or glass resin. In the past, must would ferment in wooden vats open at the top: technology, in the wake of scientific research, has taken huge steps in the past decades to the benefit of wine quality and a better organization of work in the winery.

PUMPING OVER: an operation in which liquid from the bottom portion of the fermentation vat is transported through tubes to the upper portion of the vat to spray and wet the cap of marc. This operation is done with hand-operated pumps or, preferably, with a computerized system to automatically perform several pumping-over operations per day for each vat.

"At this point we have finished the phase that uses the most modern technology and we are entering the part of the winery where the premium wines are kept to mature in wooden **casks** or in **barriques**. The length of time will vary depending on the type of wine we wish to obtain." The rooms are immersed in half-light, while the long rows of casks and barriques create a magical atmosphere. The explanations on the importance of these containers capture everyone's attention. It is almost like a mystery film: you could hear a pin drop... No, it almost seems that you can hear the wine breathing as it rests in the barrels...

As a matter of fact, wood is a porous material and the wine contained in casks or barriques really does breathe – and rest – through its pores. The action of oxygen from air that filters from the exterior through the pores, and the components of the wood itself, are very strategic. Both contribute to maturing the wine, conferring a specific and particular flavour, for example, of vanilla. Just like the one that we can smell clearly now, within the **cask cellar** and **barrique cellar**.

Here we find Vincenzo, the wine-maker, who has just begun checking the climatic conditions of the rooms and the wine. "We must guarantee optimal temperature and humidity so that the wine inside the barriques will be preserved in the best possible way". The size, age and type of wood the barriques are made of are all factors that strongly influence the final result.

Speaking of barriques, the teacher can't resist and adds a historical note, "The term 'barricade' comes from the use of barriques filled with earth or stones to create road barriers during the French Revolution!"

Francesco's mum adds another detail about the casks: "In the past, monasteries used to have very large casks because they would produce wine for the monks and for the many poor people who would request charity. At that time, in fact, wine was consumed in great quantities because it provides energy and often substituted food which was scarce".

But stories and digressions don't distract the students from their wine journey begun with the bunches they personally picked to produce a premium wine. That's why it will be aged in wooden casks for about one year. If it were a simpler wine, it would have been sufficient to vinify it in stainless steel and then bottle it.

A BIT OF RELIGION

IN THE CHRISTIAN FAITH, WINE AND GRAPES ARE RECURRING SYMBOLIC ELEMENTS. AS EARLY AS IN THE FIRST BOOK OF THE BIBLE, THE GENESIS, THERE IS THE STORY OF NOAH WHO – AFTER THE FLOOD – PLANTED THE FIRST VINE AND THEN BECAME DRUNK WITH THE JUICE OF ITS FRUIT. THE VINE IS A SYMBOL OF PROSPERITY AND OF GOD'S LOVE: WINE IS TRANSFORMED INTO THE BLOOD OF CHRIST AND THE VINEYARD IS OFTEN RECALLED AS A METAPHOR OF ISRAEL AND OF THE ENTIRE CHURCH. THERE ARE HUNDREDS OF REFERENCES TO THE VINE AND TO WINE IN THE OLD AND NEW TESTAMENTS. IT IS INTERESTING TO NOTE THAT, IN JEWISH CULTURE, THE TREE OF PARADISE IS NOT THE APPLE TREE, BUT THE VINE.

BARRIQUES: wooden containers, generally in oak, used for ageing and sometimes for fermenting wine. They are made of curved planks – staves – with two flat extremities and are held together by iron rings. They conventionally hold 225 litres of wine. The term is French since it is typical of the Bordeaux growing area in France. The Italian term – *carati* or *caratelli* – is used less often. In order to ensure that wine and wood interact in the right way, it is preferable to use a barrique for no more than four times. Therefore, for a uniform quality, the set of barriques must be renewed according to a four-year cycle of rotation, to have the same running percentage of new and older ones. So, for an optimal use, each year 25% of the barriques is discarded and substituted with the same number of new barriques. They could still be used after four passages, but with results of lesser quality. Finally, it is worth noting that the smaller the cask, the greater the ratio of surface to volume and therefore, the greater the oxygenation of the contents. Consequently, the wine needs to stay for a shorter time compared to one stored in a larger cask. The most commonly used wood is oak, particularly French oak. One cubic metre of oak produces about 6 barriques.

BARRIQUE CELLAR: is the room where the barriques are stored: to protect them from sudden temperature changes, the room is air conditioned so that the temperature remains around 14 °C (57 °F) and humidity is constant at about 65-70%.

CASK: larger than a barrique, it can be found in various sizes or capacities. Nowadays, casks are much smaller than in the past because they are easier to use and maintain, also because the wine matured in them is better. On average, a cask contains 50 hectolitres and is kept in use for no more than 20-25 years during which – every 8-10 years – it is internally "scraped" to renew the porosity of the wood because tartrates – wine salts – deposit on the internal surfaces, obstructing the pores.

CASK CELLAR: the room where casks are stored.

End of story? Not quite! The wine still has excessive **acidity**. At this point, the **lactic bacteria** can enter into action and produce a second fermentation called **malolactic fermentation**, "softening" the wine and making the flavour more elegant while transforming **malic acid** into **lactic acid**. The lactic bacteria – a veritable army! – set to work when the temperature begins to rise, after the winter, and it is the duty of the cellar-master to do everything possible to favour its initiation. For this reason, it is good to warm up the cellar where the wine – which has to undergo this second fermentation – is stored in casks and barriques. It would be a problem if malolactic fermentation were to occur when the wine is already bottled, because it ends up cloudy and bubbly! Francesco's mum remembers one of her trips to the United States and tells the story of an important winery in the Napa Valley in California, where she saw a large stainless steel vat wrapped in an electric blanket, "It was a slightly crazy, but ingenious method devised by an imaginative enologist in order to heat the wine in the vat to start up the malolactic fermentation despite the particularly cold weather". Get the lesson? Never give up when faced with the unexpected!

The wine remains in observation even afterwards, during its resting period. And it's Marco who goes to check on it occasionally, making sure that everything is proceeding well, while Vincenzo, carefully, makes regular checks on the wine with laboratory testing. It's always better to check and be sure that the wine is not deteriorating. The cask must always be kept full so that air doesn't enter it, otherwise the wine would become damaged, or – as we say – it would become oxidized. Should the internal level of the wine decrease, it is immediately topped up to prevent the air from entering and damaging the work of so many people.

That part of the cellar is in half-light, away from direct light so as not to "disturb" the wine and also later – after being bottled – the wine must stay in the dark at cool temperatures. Isn't it true that we rest better in the dark, too?

A BIT OF RELIGION

ISLAM DOES NOT ADMIT WINE CONSUMPTION, BUT IN THE KORAN, WINE IS NOT ALWAYS JUDGED NEGATIVELY. ACCORDING TO SOME HISTORIANS, HOWEVER, IT IS STIGMATIZED - LIKE ALL ALCOHOLIC BEVERAGES - PERHAPS DUE TO THE ENVIRONMENT IN WHICH THE ISLAMIC RELIGION ORIGINATED AND DEVELOPED. IN HOT AND DRY TERRITORIES SUCH AS THE DESERT, ANY ALCOHOLIC BEVERAGE WAS CONSIDERED DANGEROUS TO THE HEALTH OF THE PEOPLE AND, THEREFORE, INSIDIOUS FOR BALANCE WITHIN THE NOMADIC COMMUNITIES. BETTER, THEREFORE, TO AVOID IT.

ACIDITY: one of the ways to evaluate the structure of a wine. A good wine must have good acidity from the beginning, especially if it must undergo malolactic fermentation (see below) which will lower it. The final acidity can also be influenced by vinification techniques. If the initial acidity, which depends on climate and the grape's degree of ripeness, is too low, the final one will not be enough. Therefore, the wine will not have body and will seem flat. If it is too high, the wine will be hard and acidic, unbalanced, and will have an excessively sour and sharp flavour. Acids are fundamental for the final balance and prevent the wine from deteriorating during fermentation and aging. It is interesting to note that acidity is perceived along the sides of the mouth and tongue.

LACTIC ACID: a "weak" acid. It is so called because it is the same acid which makes milk curdle.

LACTIC BACTERIA: micro-organisms naturally present in wine, already found in the bloom (page 7) that covers the grape. The Latin name is *Lactobacillus*.

MALIC ACID: a "strong" acid present principally in unripe apples, sambuco, black-currants and in grapes that are not yet ripe.

MALOLACTIC FERMENTATION OR **SECONDARY FERMENTATION:** an essential process for the biological stability of wines caused by lactic bacteria which provoke the degradation of malic acid into lactic acid and carbon dioxide. It helps reduce the sharpness (typical of malic acid) and makes the wine softer (lactic acid is much less aggressive than malic acid) with more complex and "mature" aromas. Malolactic fermentation is indispensable for the quality of red wines, in which it is always favoured, and in some white wines. It must not, on the other hand, occur in fresh white, rosé and those red wines where we prefer the freshness of the acidity and the "youthful" aromas of fruit and flowers. The most practical and simple method for preventing it is to obstruct the activity of the lactic bacteria by adding a suitable dose of sulphur dioxide to the wine or – by far the best method – by keeping the wine at low temperature.

We are close to the wire, but right at the end, before the wine is bottled, there is one more exam. Just as our grandparents often say: you never finish being put to the test.

This particular one makes a final judgement on the work done, awaited but dreaded at the same time: the **organoleptic exam** (pages 41 and 59) of the wine by a commission of tasters who verify the quality of the wine and determine how well it corresponds to the requirements. There are several tasters on the panel, because the evaluation must be an objective and shared one. It is a demanding one because its goal is quality, but it must also take into account that the wine is still not complete, at this stage. After filtering and bottling, it will mature even more before reaching the consumer. So, the tasters take into consideration the work that has already been done and make a forecast on the future product. "But it's that way, even at school!" exclaim the students, who have attentively followed all the explanations. "There is always an examining board that, after the testing done by our teacher, could give you a failing grade: does the wine get to repeat the exam?"

Vincenzo smiles, amused at the idea of having the wine (or the grapes) "repeat the year", and jokes that, since he is such a good technician, the wine can only choose between getting a "very good" or a "good" grade! When the tasting commission announces its verdict, he will then blend, or assemble, the contents of all those barrels and barriques that the students now see. The process of producing one large flow of wine from many barrels is called blending.

We have finally reached the finish line: the wine is now ready to move on to the **filtration** stage which will remove the **lees** and, finally, **bottling**. "There could also be" says Vicenzo, "an alternative technique to definitively stabilize the wine called **pasteurization**, but it is used only for mass-production wines, never for quality ones".

ANECDOTE

ACCORDING TO SOME HISTORIANS, THE TERM "WINE" COULD DERIVE FROM THE SANSCRIT WORD *VENA* WHICH MEANS "TO LOVE" (FROM WHICH THE NAME VENUS; THIS WOULD CONFIRM THE GREAT APPRECIATION FOR THIS DRINK RIGHT FROM THE BEGINNING!). THE LATIN *VINUM* HAS BECOME *WEIN* IN GERMAN; *WIJN* IN DUTCH; *VIN* IN SWEDISH, DANISH AND FRENCH; *VINHO* IN PORTUGUESE AND, FINALLY, *VINO* IN SPANISH AND ITALIAN!

BOTTLING: an operation requiring great attention that must be carried out in a sterile environment. The wine is bottled only after having undergone all the necessary stabilization and filtering processes. Before filling the bottle, a machine inserts nitrogen in the gaseous state: this pushes out the oxygen naturally present in the air that could cause the wine to oxidise if it were to remain in the bottle neck.

FILTRATION: an operation consisting in separating the wine from the "fine lees" still suspended in it.

LEES: the last solid particles deriving from fermentation dispersed in the liquid. They give flavour and consistency to the wine, but must be eliminated during decantation and with a final filtering process, resulting in a clear wine.

ORGANOLEPTIC EXAMINATION: the wine test according to the three parameters: visual, olfactory, gustative (taste). While the laboratory test reveals possible defects in the chemical constitution, the organoleptic exam not only defines the goodness of the wine, but above all verifies if it responds to certain typical characteristics such as those of the area of origin (for a detailed description of sensorial analysis, see page 59).

PASTEURIZATION: a technique developed by Louis Pasteur used for preserving wine for longer periods by heating it to 57 °C (135 °F) for a few minutes. This eliminates the micro-organisms responsible for acidification and deterioration of wine. It is only valid for low-quality wines or wines not to be aged, because in order to make them sterile, the process strips them of flavour.

In a winery such as the one we are visiting, almost all operations are automatized. It is fascinating to see the long line of **bottles** being transported by a conveyor belt, going under the bottling machine, then on to the machine that shoots the cork into the bottle neck. All those bottles parading with a happy, tinkling sound really look like little soldiers marching!

Now Francesco's mum becomes serious and asks the students to be careful and not touch the bottles as they pass by. "There are many safety mechanisms, but everyone would be sorry if one of the more lively students were to end up inside a bottle, looking out at the teacher and fellow classmates with his nose crushed up against the glass!" The students have a good laugh at that and are ready again to hear about corks. They realize that to seal a bottle one can use closures of various materials: the most common are **natural corks**, but there are also **synthetic corks** and even **screw-caps**, **glass caps** and **crown caps** that can be used for wines.

The story of grapes that become wine is not finished, however: while fresher wines would be immediately bottled, let's remember that our journey has followed the vinification of a premium red wine that needs a long refining period.

BOTTLES: must be made of glass, a material that does not interact with wine, inert, rigid and impermeable, all qualities required for keeping a long time. Wines for ageing are generally stored in dark-coloured bottles that protect from the light. There are numerous shapes and sizes (for more details, go to page 69). The alternative to glass is tetra-pack or "bag-in-box" (aluminium or plastic bags), but until now these have not been associated with quality wines, although they are quite common in Northern Europe and undoubtedly practical. This type of packaging is being taken into consideration by some producers for simple wines that are not for ageing.

NATURAL CORK: obtained from the bark of a special variety of oak tree (an evergreen tree, botanical term: *Quercus suber*). In the past, other materials were used, such as parchment, oakum, fabric soaked in oil, etc. Nowadays, corks are the only closures using natural materials. They can be either whole or pressed from chips glued together. To avoid the entry of air during bottle ageing and storage, the bottle should be kept horizontal so that the wine wets the cork and dilates it to the maximum. The cork could present – and this unfortunately happens, sometimes! – some tiny tunnels inside that are invisible from the exterior through which the wine can find its way and perhaps cause mould formation. These cause an unpleasant "corked" smell and taste which irreparably damage the contents of the entire bottle. For this reason, when opening a bottle, we should immediately smell the cork to be certain about the wine quality. And if the cork is "polluted", the only solution is unfortunately to throw away the bottle or send it back, if at a restaurant.

GLASS CAPS: adhere to the bottle neck thanks to a silicon ring. They are quite costly and not very common.

SCREW-CAP AND **CROWN CAP:** technically speaking, the caps that guarantee the best seal for bottled wine by completely inhibiting the passage of air. They are not used often, however; especially the crown cap is generally not used for quality wines.

SYNTHETIC CORKS: produced with artificial materials, generally plastic polymers. They also come in various colours, but are not suitable for premium wines and above all do not guarantee a good closure for many years as opposed to natural corks. Therefore, they are only suitable for wines to be drunk young.

Once bottled, our wine must still rest in a **refining** cellar, a room with a soft atmosphere. The bottles laid down in rows give the idea of a group of elves resting: even here it seems that we can hear the sound of the wine breathing while immersed in who-knows-what kind of fantastic dreams...

We are not far away from the truth in thinking that the wine is sleeping: wine is in fact a "living" food, very sensitive to the characteristics of the surrounding environment and, therefore, after the stress of vinification and bottling, it needs a rest period ranging from a few days to several years, according to its type and quality. At the end, when woken up from its sleep, the wine will be even more elegant and refined than when it entered. And it will be almost ready to reach the tables of its friends and connoisseurs.

"Almost ready?! But, what's left to do?!" the students ask, impatiently.

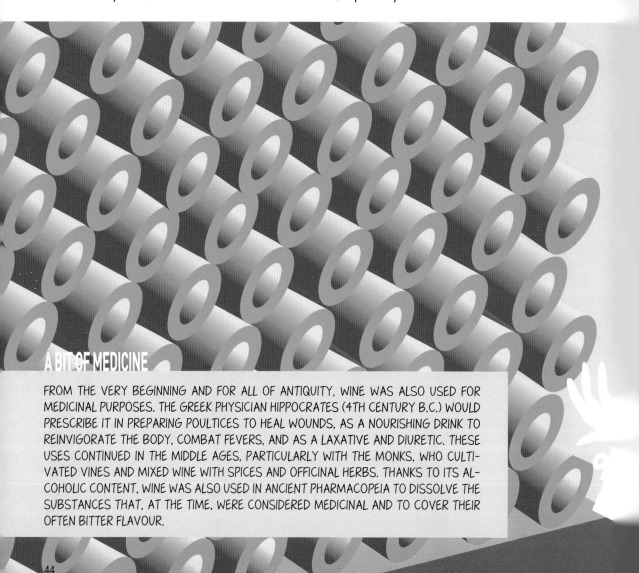

A BIT OF MEDICINE

FROM THE VERY BEGINNING AND FOR ALL OF ANTIQUITY, WINE WAS ALSO USED FOR MEDICINAL PURPOSES. THE GREEK PHYSICIAN HIPPOCRATES (4TH CENTURY B.C.) WOULD PRESCRIBE IT IN PREPARING POULTICES TO HEAL WOUNDS, AS A NOURISHING DRINK TO REINVIGORATE THE BODY, COMBAT FEVERS, AND AS A LAXATIVE AND DIURETIC. THESE USES CONTINUED IN THE MIDDLE AGES, PARTICULARLY WITH THE MONKS, WHO CULTIVATED VINES AND MIXED WINE WITH SPICES AND OFFICINAL HERBS. THANKS TO ITS ALCOHOLIC CONTENT, WINE WAS ALSO USED IN ANCIENT PHARMACOPEIA TO DISSOLVE THE SUBSTANCES THAT, AT THE TIME, WERE CONSIDERED MEDICINAL AND TO COVER THEIR OFTEN BITTER FLAVOUR.

REFINING: the transformations that wine undergoes in barrel and in bottle. As the word implies, the wine further improves, matures and acquires elegance: for this reason, after bottling, the bottles must be kept laid down in ideal temperatures (between 10 and 14 °C (50-57 °F), humidity (80% relative humidity) and with little light. In the winery, the characteristics of a refining cellar are recreated artificially. These are also recommended for a home wine cellar and even more so for restaurant cellars, keeping in mind that heat, odours and vibrations are enemies of wine. The time required for a good refining period varies depending on the type of wine and is reserved only for premium wines. For example, for a Torgiano Rosso Riserva DOCG or a Barolo DOCG, this lasts for many years, allowing the consumer to purchase a product with great softness.

Well, seeing those dusty bottles of wine resting in the cellar, it is easy to understand that before leaving the winery they must be thoroughly washed by a washing machine, dried with cold air and then go through the labeling machine to "be dressed" in **labels** (would you ever go out without washing and dressing?!). Lastly, the cork will be covered with a **capsule**.

Finally, the bottles are ready to reach their destination. They will travel – grouped together in cardboard boxes (the piles of cartons form multicoloured walls!) or in wooden cases – and be shipped all over the world: in Europe and to America, Asia, even as far as Australia.

For this reason, the labels have Italian and English indications. It is Franzoil, the purchasing manager, who procures all the materials required to ship wine all over the world. Among his many responsibilities, he must check that the labels, cartons and wooden cases all have the mandatory mentions, such as "contains **sulphites**" as well as the vintage year, or year of production. Speaking of Franzoil: his real name is Francesco, but since he is an expert on olive oil – a product from central Italy often associated with wine – his colleagues have re-named him "Franzoil": his nickname has a good ring to it and there are so many people who use it that, occasionally, when he meets someone for the first time, he inadvertently gives his nickname. "Let's read a label together" he suggests, showing a bottle just labelled. Easy, but let's follow together.

1. Producer's name or brand name;
2. Product brand name or varietal name;
3. Place name of a sub-area of the territory (not mandatory). In this case, the name of the vineyard where the grapes come from;
4. Appellation: indicated in full and not abbreviated; or V.Q.P.R.D., the European Union abbreviation indicating a Quality Wine Produced in Specified Regions (not obligatory, it corresponds to the Italian DOC or DOCG); the term Riserva is only used if the production legislation allows it and only for aged wines;
5. Year of production, mandatory under the Appellation;
6. Official company name of the winery, city and country where the wine is bottled;
7. Alcoholic strength;
8. Country of Origin;
9. Capacity of the container; the **e** is a European symbol guaranteeing the bottle capacity;
10. Mandatory mention; if the wine is to be exported, it must be written in the language of the importing country. It indicates that the wine contains more than 10 mg/litre of sulphur dioxide;
11. The bottling lot number: (can be indicated on the label or on the capsule), essential for tracing the product.

Wine lovers know which years correspond to the best harvests of the most well known wine areas: never heard James Bond, secret agent 007, order with great savoir-faire a "Dom Pérignon 1953"?

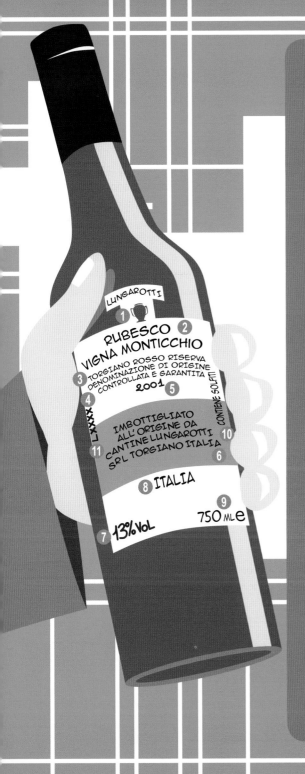

CAPSULE: an accessory of fundamental importance. Premium wines always have a capsule that covers the cork: its principle function is to avoid dust deposits, the formation of moulds, or insects from entering the cork. It also slows down the air/wine exchange, but has three tiny holes in the top to prevent mould-producing humidity. In general, capsules are in tinfoil; the ones in polylaminate (aluminium between two layers of plastic) and in heat-shrink plastic are more economical. Some producers use a red wax seal instead of the capsule, but this is costly and not very practical.

LABEL: a sort of wine "identity card", fundamental because it supplies all the information about origin, type, appellation, alcoholic strength, vintage year and, above all, the name of the producer, which is the greatest guarantee. On the labels of premium wines there is also an indication of the appellation (such as IGT, DOC, etc., see page 65). Not obligatory, but useful for the consumer is the back label opposite the main one that describes the wine: varietals used, recommended food matchings, serving temperature, bar code, etc.

SULPHITES OR **SULFITES**: anti-oxidant substances derived from sulphur dioxide (chemical formula SO^2), a gas with a sharp odour. The addition of sulphites serves to control the vinification and protect the wine from oxidation. Good enological techniques tend to reduce the use of sulphites as much as possible to make the wine more digestible and avoid annoying traces: that's why it is important to have the healthiest possible grapes under a hygienic-sanitary perspective and the use of cold temperatures during vinification.

"What an exciting overview: now we know much more about wine and we're eager to be considered wine experts!" exclaims the teacher, who has become just as curious as the students. "We know that wine is defined as *an alcoholic beverage obtained from the total or partial fermentation of grapes*, but we can imagine that there are still thousands more secrets in the use of it, for example, how to store and enjoy it. We would love to make a good impression if someone asked us to distinguish wines according to their characteristics, besides colour. Could you tell us how to do it?"

As she looks over the group of attentive and curious youngsters with satisfaction, Francesco's mum confirms: "It is always impressive when you can talk about wine with competence; even more so when you have mastered the art of matching wine with food. "And as you become experts, your vocabulary will be enriched with terms such as *Soft*, *Mellow*, *Medium-dry*, *Balanced*, *Harmonious*, *Alluring*, *Amiable*, *Sapid*, *Full-bodied*, *Meaty*, *Vigorous*, *Round*, *Tart*, *Aggressive* and more: appropriate words to describe the wine you have in your glass!

It is very satisfying to identify the right combinations between food and wine, be it **white**, **red** or **rosé** and be able to choose the most suitable ones for drinking as an aperitif before the meal. I recommend" says Francesco's mum "never drinking on an empty stomach! The best way to appreciate a wine is to sip it slowly, without exceeding the limits, and best of all, enjoy it in good company!"

A separate thought goes to "special wines", the ones that undergo particular treatments: **Novello**, **Spumante**, **lightly sparkling wines (*Frizzante*)**, **Passito** wines (made with semi-dried grapes) or **"wines for meditation"**, **sweet wines from noble rot**, **ice-wines** or ***Eiswein***, **fortified wines**, and **aromatised wines** (see pages 50-51).

And to finish off, not a new type of wine, but a special drink made with red wine aromatised with spices and served very hot, just as the Medieval monks used to prepare, knowing the health properties of wine, spices and wild herbs: **mulled wine** or *vin brûlé* ("burnt wine" in French). Steaming, spicy and healthy, it is a home-made remedy that is both food and medication, delicious and excellent for fighting a cold! Let's discover together its strengthening, warming and disinfecting properties.

IN THE KITCHEN

LET'S NOT FORGET THAT WINE IS ALSO AN EXCELLENT IN-GREDIENT IN COOKING: FROM APPETIZERS TO DESSERTS, IT IS A FRIEND OF GREAT CHEFS BECAUSE OF THE CREATIVITY THAT IT HELPS THEM EXPRESS IN THEIR DISHES. IN ADDITION TO ENHANCING FOOD-WINE PAIRINGS, WINE IS USED IN PREPARING DISHES, FOR MARINATING MEAT, BRAISING FOOD IN SAUCEPANS AND EVEN FOR PREPARING SAUCES. THERE ARE EVEN SHERBETS AND ICE CREAMS MADE WITH WINE.

A "TASTY" NATURAL MEDICATION: MULLED WINE OR VIN BRÛLÉ

If your dad has gotten a cold and begins sneezing, let's revive the recipe from the monks for "cooked wine" to lift both body and spirit during the long, dark Medieval winters. "A litre of red wine, 300 gr (7/8 cup) of honey, preferably of strawberry-tree or acacia, 2 cinnamon sticks, 3 cloves. Boil the wine over low heat with all the ingredients until it is reduced to one third. Drink hot."
It is not difficult to make and, even if you are not a perfect cook, the result is guaranteed and your dad will be very grateful!

WHITE WINE comes from white grapes, or from red grapes using "white vinification". The yellow colour can be of varying tones: from greenish to amber, through shades of straw-yellow and golden. Ideal for fish-based dishes, shellfish and crustaceans, vegetables and white meats. Fresh, young white wines produced in stainless steel are also often used as aperitifs.

ROSÉ WINE comes from red grapes that undergo a brief maceration and its colour can be various tones of pink, from pale salmon to a stronger raspberry pink. It matches very well with more savoury fish dishes, pasta with delicate sauces, legumes, light-flavoured cured meats and egg-based dishes.

RED WINE comes from red grapes vinified with a long maceration and can come in many shades: from purple to ruby up to garnet. When aged, it tends to take on a more evocative brick shade. The ideal companion for red meats – the more robust ones – match well with game and aged cheeses. The matchings, however, can vary greatly depending on the "body" of the wine.

NOVELLO: a red, young and lively wine. The premiere wine of the harvest, obtained from carbonic maceration (page 25) and characterized by fragrant scents of strawberry, raspberry and bilberry, as well as an intense, fruity bouquet and particularly brilliant colour with purple hues. It is released on the market, according to legislation, on November 6th following the harvest and is consumed within the winter months to fully appreciate its bouquet. Every year, on the eve of the release, there is a celebration (*déblocage*, as the French call it, as they have the same celebration with their Beaujolais Nouveau, on the third Wednesday of November). Novello has the characteristics of a young wine, so it matches very well with dishes having delicate flavours and the traditional roasted chestnuts.

SPUMANTE: the bubbly wines used for toasting on special occasions. The effervescence – or *perlage*, in French – is caused by the CO_2 produced according to two different methods:

SPECIAL WINES

In **Metodo Classico**, also called "traditional method" (or *Champenoise*, referring only to the sparkling wines produced in the Champagne area in France. In Spain the method is called *Cava* or *Tradicional*; in Italy, Metodo Classico), the CO_2 is naturally released during the process of alcoholic re-fermentation of the wine in bottle, previously enriched with a syrup containing yeasts and sugar – *liqueur de tirage*. The bottles, sealed with crown caps, remain for months in the horizontal position for taking on the sparkle, that is another fermentation. The bottles are then placed neck-down in turning frames (*pupitres*) and, each day, they are turned and inclined (*remouage*, or shaking) so that the residues of the fermentation will gradually precipitate towards the bottle neck; at the end the bottle remains *sur la pointe*, upside down, until the disgorgement (*dégorgement*), when the neck is immersed into a refrigerating liquid, so that the residues located at the bottle neck will solidify and be easily removed. By opening the bottle, the internal pressure makes the cap of ice pop out. The wine removed by disgorgement is topped up with a syrup, called *liqueur d'expedition*, composed of wine, brown sugar and cognac. Next is corking, with the mushroom-shaped cork and wire muzzle. The release of foam when you uncork the bottle is due to the high internal CO_2 pressure (minimum 3.5 atmospheres, 6 on average). Spumante can be sweet or dry, with a series of intermediate levels: *Pas Dosé, Dosage Zéro, Nature, Extra Brut, Brut, Extra Dry, Dry, Medium-Dry, Doux* (sweet). For centuries, the origin of the method was attributed to the Benedectine monk Dom Perignon. Recently documents have been discovered in which it appears that an Italian physician, Francesco Scacchi, had described this method many years earlier, in 1622.

The **Charmat Method** also produces CO_2 from the fermentation of a wine to which a syrup of yeasts and sugar has been added. Not in bottle, but in large vats with airtight seals and temperature control called "autoclaves" that can withstand the strong pressure of the CO_2 in the wine. This process is fast and cheap, so it is suitable for wines not requiring a long ageing period. The origin of this method is cause of controversy: an Italian enologist, Federico Martinotti, was the first to devise this system at the end of the 1800's, but the French producer Charmat was the first to use it on an industrial scale in the early 1900's.

LIGHTLY SPARKLING WINES: these wines, with less pressure than Spumante, do not require wire muzzles, heavy-duty bottles or special closures. They are obtained from natural fermentation in autoclaves for just a few months or by adding CO_2 before bottling. In this case, it is obligatory to indicate "CO_2 added" on the label. They are lively and fresh wines, particularly appreciated as aperitifs.

PASSITO OR **"MEDITATION WINES"**: made from grapes that are left on the vine to become over-ripe (late harvest) and naturally dry out, or picked and spread onto drying racks or hung in aerated rooms so they do not produce mould. The drying out causes a high sugar concentration, so Passito wines are sweet wines to be matched with desserts. Wine connoisseurs also love to accompany them with cheeses and foie-gras. They are also called "meditation wines" because they are very pleasant to drink between meals.

SWEET WINES FROM NOBLE ROT: obtained from botritized grapes that have been attacked by the noble rot called Botrytis Cinerea which penetrates into the berry and enriches it with a precious aromatic range. In order to develop this particular mould – which is not the same one caused by rain and hot-humid weather, but is a "noble" one – it is necessary that vines grow in a particular climate alternating between foggy and dry conditions.

FORTIFIED WINES: produced using a base wine of at least 12% alcohol content enriched with wine-alcohol and a concentrate of must to increase the alcohol content up to 16% in order to inhibit the yeasts: in this way the wine can remain sweet without the risk of the residual sugar's refermenting. Fortified wine can be released to the market without wood ageing, but a barrique-refining period gives it added value. The most famous fortified wines are: Port and Marsala, from wine+alcohol and must; while Madeira and Sherry (Jerez/Xeres) are produced with must+alcohol. These wines are good matches for desserts, cheeses and foie-gras.

ICE WINE AND **EISWEIN:** wines produced in the cold regions of Canada or the USA (the former) and in Germany or Austria (the latter). They are produced with over-ripe grapes whose water content has frozen at the sub-zero temperatures generally reached in the winter months in these areas. During pressing, the water remains crystallized in the skins and the resulting juice is more concentrated and richer in sugars. So, each vine produces approximately one-fifth of the wine that could have been obtained otherwise: about the contents of one glass of wine.

AROMATISED WINES: their flavour is determined by the addition of alcohol, sugar – or must – and natural extracts, with a minimum alcohol content of 10%. These are not to be confused with aromatic wines that are regular wines obtained from grapes that are naturally aromatic (Moscato, Gewurtztraminer, etc.). Vermouth and Barolo Chinato (with china-berry) are aromatised wines.

The "professor-mum" adds that when they grow up, Francesco and his friends could become proficient wine tasters, perhaps even professional **sommeliers**: yes, the ones with the typical uniform (of which they feel so proud!) and the **taste-vin** around their necks. Or even enologists: after all, with a visit like this one, they are already budding enologists, possessing knowledge that others don't have. However, even if, as adults, their relationship with wine may not be professional, but simply a source of enjoyment, it will be interesting and pleasant not only to appreciate but, above all, to be able to recognize a wine. So, now is the time to begin cultivating one's sense of smell and taste: it will certainly be very useful. They will need to be able to distinguish scents and flavours of flowers, fruit, berries, enriching their olfactory and gustative memory, as well as develop their own **taste**. She recommends eating healthy foods, possibly in season. And pay attention to how the food is prepared and with which ingredients: this way one can better memorize flavours and be able to identify the best matchings between food and wine, enhancing both. On the other hand, if the "marriage" is not successful, there is no pleasure nor satisfaction. Above all, let's never forget that a good wine gives pleasure and should be enjoyed with the proper appreciation for this magnificent gift of nature and of the work of man, that deserves, once again, happiness and respect!

TIP

The important thing to always remember is to drink with moderation and to drink a good wine; otherwise instead of doing us good, it could damage the liver. Better to have one less sip, but of better quality: it will be an advantage for your taste, health and good humour.

TASTE-VIN

A BIT OF CULTURE

THE VINE, GRAPES AND WINE ARE ALSO THE BASIS OF MANY PROVERBS AND ADAGES "DISTILLED" FROM ANCIENT POPULAR WISDOM. THEY APPEAR IN TRADITIONAL SONGS, CLASSICAL OPERA AND EVEN POP SONGS. NOWADAYS, JUST A CLICK OF THE COMPUTER GIVES US AN IMMEDIATE LINK, BUT LET'S NOT FORGET THE PLEASURE OF LEAFING THROUGH BOOKS IN WHICH WE CAN LEARN ABOUT THE IMPORTANCE OF WINE: NOT ONLY IN SCIENCE OR IN FOODS, BUT ALSO IN THE IMAGINATION AND IN CULTURE: AS WE CAN SEE, BOTH IN THE VISUAL ARTS AND IN LITERATURE.

SOMMELIER: a professional who is an expert on wine, able to evaluate its type, quality, characteristics, assets and possible defects and above all, to find the proper wine-food pairings. At a restaurant, wine shop or bar, the sommelier makes recommendations and consults with the consumer, then begins the operations that are part of a rite: uncorking the wine, controlling its colour and brilliantness and smelling the cork to make sure there are no unpleasant smells; tasting it in his special silver tasting cup and finally serving it, taking care to choose the suitable glass to highlight colour, bouquet and flavour. To become a sommelier one must attend special courses.

TASTE: term that indicates one of the five senses and, at the same time, the set of sensations one perceives in the mouth, connected to the senses of flavour and smell, as well as tactile and thermal stimulus. During wine tasting (as we will see in greater detail on page 59) the taste of a wine is cataloged on the basis of various parameters:
acidity (vivacious flavour);
sweetness (degree of sweetness);
harmony (the right balance between the various components);
alcohol (alcoholic content);
age (the state of its evolution);
body (from all the components of the wine except volatile compounds);
softness (relationship between sweetness and acidity);
persistence in the mouth (even after having swallowed);
tannicity (a characteristic of red wines only).

TASTE-VIN ("tasting cup" in French): a small, wide vessel in silver suspended on a chain and worn by professional sommeliers around the neck. It is used to taste the wine before serving it. The inside has small indentations where the wine is collected and reflects the light so the sommelier can judge colour and clarity.

To appreciate wine properly, you definitely need two or three things: the first is, as already mentioned, an appropriate **pairing with food** (page 49 and page 55). The second is the correct **serving temperature**. Each type of wine has its own. But be careful of the external temperature, too: leaving wine in the sun or close to a source of heat would make it warm up and become ruined. If it is too cold, on the other hand, the flavour will not be the "usual" one and the pleasure in drinking it will be greatly reduced.

For the maximum enjoyment, you also need the right glass: the best type is a thin stem-glass (or the more prized crystal) not coloured, nor decorated. The glass can be of different shapes (see page 67) according to the various wine types, and designed to facilitate the meeting of the wine with the drinker's **taste buds**. To experience the sensations even more intensely, a little trick: the aroma released by the wine in the glass is enhanced even more if the glass is just one-third full. This way the wine can be swirled in the glass to oxygenate it as much as possible: a movement that requires a bit of practice before you can do it with confidence and elegance and without risking... stains on tablecloths and clothing of the people sitting next to you! "But if a little accident does happen?" asks the teacher, worried yet curious (answer at bottom of page).

To appreciate red wine in the best way, in some cases it can be "decanted", poured into a special wine jug (decanter) to let it breathe. This way it can release its aroma when coming into contact with the air, especially if it has been sealed in the bottle for a long time. Just think of how you feel when stepping out into the fresh air and taking a deep breath: this is what happens to wine. Decanting is also useful for separating the wine from sediments that could form with ageing. In this case the wine must be poured without shaking it, so that the deposits remain at the bottom. For this operation the light of a candle could also be useful.

SERVING TEMPERATURE
Red wines: 16 to 18 °C (60-64 °F, room temperature)
Rosés: 14 °C (57 °F)
Whites: 8 to 12 °C (46-54 °F)
Spumante or **Champagne** – in a word, bubbles: 8 to 10 °C (46-50 °F)

TIP
To remove a red wine stain, sprinkle it with salt and wash in hot water. If red wine gets on the tablecloth, try to dry it immediately with a napkin. Then put another clean napkin under the tablecloth, pour a bit of white wine on the stain and let the stain become soaked. Finally, rinse very well with warm water.

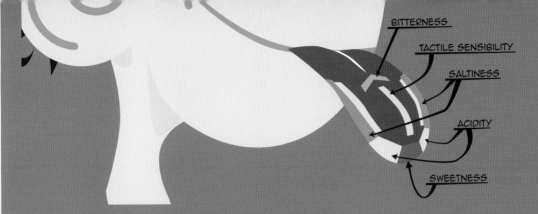

BITTERNESS

TACTILE SENSIBILITY

SALTINESS

ACIDITY

SWEETNESS

TASTE BUDS: the sensors of the tongue that perceive gustative and tactile sensations and transmit them to the brain. We have about 3,000 of them, diversified according to function. The drawing represents the "map" of the areas on the tongue where various tastes are perceived: sweetness at the tip, bitterness at the back, while acidity and saltiness are perceived along the sides. The central part of the tongue feels tactile sensations such as:

astringency, from the combination of young tannins with the proteins of the saliva which then loses its lubricating power;

sharpness, barely perceptible, due to the carbon dioxide produced during malolactic fermentation

effervescence, from the carbon dioxide in sparkling wines;

heat, or rather, a heat-like sensation (not to be confused with the thermal sensation) is the dehydration caused by the presence of alcohol; it is generally rounded out by the acidity of the wine.

Taste buds also perceive thermal sensations: hot and cold. These can influence tactile sensations: for example, sweetness and softness are more perceptible as the temperature rises, while coldness makes astringency and alcohol content less perceptible.

FOOD PAIRING, OR TO EACH DISH ITS WINE...

Appetizers: whites and rosés, light and delicate, or dry Spumante

Seafood, oysters, salmon, crustaceans: dry whites or dry Spumante

Soups: dry whites with higher alcohol content

Pasta dishes: if the sauce is fish-based, dry white; if meat-based, reds that are not too robust; if game-based, generous dry reds

Fish and seafood: dry whites from fresh to structured, according to the intensity of flavour of the fish

White meat roasts, poultry, boiled meats: generous and soft reds, not too robust

Red meat roasts, game: generous and structured reds

Fried foods: if fish or vegetables, dry whites or rosés; if meat, rosés or fresh reds

Egg-based dishes or dishes with cured meats: rosés

Desserts: sweet wines, fortified wines, sweet Spumante

Salads, pickled foods, citrus fruits, artichokes: better no wine at all

Till now we have seen how to cultivate vines, obtain good grapes and vinify them. We must remember, however, that wine – especially quality wine – does not only have to be good and good for you: we also expect it to have its own, distinguishable character.

And this is where tasting comes into the picture.

Better to do it "blind", by covering the bottle to avoid being influenced by the label.

These are moving moments– especially if we taste an important wine – perhaps even an old vintage with a lot of history behind it. And here the professionals can even come up with specific expressions that often seem funny because they use a very figurative language. For example, a wine can even have "lovely legs", a colourful expression that makes us smile, describing the "tears" or "arches" that form on the glass after swirling the wine. And what would you say about a wine with an "animal scent" or that is "wise and balanced" or "sinewy", or "of good breeding", or defined with other expressions such as "tar flavour" or "underbrush flavour"?! A language that becomes almost slang, but that can precisely pinpoint a wine's characteristics.

But not to worry! A tasting can be done with less knowledge than that of an expert. On the contrary, having more personal and informal tastings can be a fun and pleasant occasion, while also being useful for beginning to deepen one's wine culture. Apart from the vocabulary used, that each person will learn by experience and on the basis of their own sensations, the wine itself will help us by telling its story and suggesting the best way to drink it. All we need to do is listen to it with our senses.

FLINTY

MEDITATION WINE

BREAD
CRUST

CHOCOLATEY

FLAVOUR OF
UNDERBRUSH

RACY

SINEWY

VISCOUS

SAVOURY,
STIMULATING
VEIN

PIPE
TOBACCO

SOFT, SILKY TEXTURE

IF IT WERE A SONG,
IT WOULD BE A LOVE SONG

"It sounds like a very complicated process, but it's actually less than it seems" assures Vincenzo, who is taking samples in the winery to bring to the tasting commission.

Using more technical terms, "tasting" means making a real **sensorial analysis** of the wine, also called **organoleptic evaluation**, because we use the senses of sight, smell and taste. The three phases are therefore: **visual**, **olfactory** and **gustative analysis**, used to perceive the quality and evolutionary stage of a wine.

For example, when we speak of scents (and there are at least 50, in wine!) the reference to flowers, fruit and spices is connected to the wine's age. We begin with young wines, therefore light and fresh scents that recall flowers and fruit, going on towards ripe fruit, jams and then dried fruit, nuts and the spicy scents evident in wines of an intermediate age, reaching the true bouquet: a symphony of scents highlighted by balsamic and dry notes (flowers, earth, leaves, hay), animal aromas, and the toasted notes of more aged and important wines. White wines are dominated by aromas that recall white and yellow flowers and fruits, while in the reds there is a prevalence of red flowers and fruits. On the other hand, each varietal has its characteristic scent: Merlot and Cabernet Sauvignon are grassy; Cabernet Sauvignon has a scent of green pepper; Syrah is peppery; Chardonnay smells of fresh butter and almond and so on. Now is it easier to understand what an olfactory memory is?

There are also defective odours: like the most common "corked" smell, caused by a fungus that attacks the cork, or the "smell of lees" connected to imperfect fermentation processes; an "oxidated smell" caused by excessive oxygenation, or a "sulphur smell" due to high sulphur dioxide content.

SENSORIAL ANALYSIS

Sensorial analysis – or organoleptic evaluation – is composed of three distinct types of analysis that together create a final judgement.

VISUAL ANALYSIS: performed by observing the wine in a transparent container, preferably against a white background; it helps form a first opinion on the quality and age of the wine, in which the following elements are evaluated:
colour (tone and intensity);
clarity or **transparency**;
consistency or **fluidity**;
effervescence (only for spumante wines, and, more specifically, quantity, consistence and persistence of the *perlage*, the flow of bubbles of carbon dioxide).

OLFACTORY ANALYSIS: this is done using the nose and, while swallowing, the retronasal passage, which is also involved, because that is where smells move from the mouth to the nose. This analysis is facilitated by swirling the glass so the wine can oxygenate and release all its bouquet. Olfactory analysis is what provides the greatest amount of information and lets us evaluate:
smell: this can be aromatic, fruity, spicy. Depending on their origin, there is a distinction between: primary aromas that come directly from the grapes; secondary aromas, that are formed by the chemical reactions during fermentation (such as the characteristic floral scent - the *bouquet* - present in the majority of white wines, or the fruity scent in reds); and, finally, tertiary aromas that are formed during the refining period (such as the characteristic scent of wood found in the wines refined in casks or in barriques);
complexity, or aromatic richness.

GUSTATIVE ANALYSIS: this is performed in the mouth through the taste buds (page 55), by taking a sip of wine and aerating it in the mouth, inhaling air and gurgling it with the wine on the sides of the tongue and not necessarily swallowing the wine. This allows the taster to evaluate many wines without running into problems of excessive alcohol.
The principle parameters of evaluation are:
body;
harmony;
intensity.

"It is still a little early for you!" Francesco's mum resumes, "but time passes quickly and, when you are older, you'll remember everything that you have seen and learned today: it will help you recognize wine as a friend to be appreciated and also respected by consuming it with the right balance".

The visit is over now: the students not only are very impressed by everything they have seen, they are even disappointed to have reached the end of such a fantastic voyage.

Francesco's mum has a surprise for everyone, though: a tasty snack and... a quiz game to reward the visitor who paid the most attention. The prize is a real cellar-man's apron! Grazia wins the prize: she's a very inquisitive girl who carefully listened to everything that was said and she proudly wears the apron, thinking that maybe when she grows up, even she could have a career in wine.

The time to return to school has arrived. In saying goodbye to the group before they board the bus, a promise: "Come back to Torgiano soon to visit the Wine Museum. It's an enchanted place for discovering a story that is five thousand years old!" says Francesco's mum, smiling and waving at the happy group.

Francesco – a future sommelier? – is very proud of this visit and his friends are already asking when they can come back: "Your mother's job is fantastic!"

THE END

IN ADDITION...

ABOUT ITALIAN WINE APPELLATIONS

Legislation number 164 (Feb. 10, 1992) divides Italian wine production into two large sections: table wines and wines with an appellation of origin – Denominazione d'origine, also indicated as VQPRD –Vini di Qualità Prodotti in Regioni Determinate (Quality wine produced in specific regions) – that are then subdivided into IGT, DOC and DOCG. These appellations are designed to give the consumer an appropriate guarantee about quality of the product and the specific requirements of typicality indicated in the production legislation. As a result of new European community legislation, No. EEC 479/2008 which became effective on August 31, 2009, a change is occurring from the IGT appellation to the new IGP, and from DOC and DOCG to DOP. Since this new classification is not yet completely defined, for now we will refer to the current IGT, DOC and DOCG appellations which figuratively and in increasing order of importance, form the

QUALITY
PYRAMID
OF WINE

The pyramid intends to describe continuously increasing quality and, therefore, value according to the classification, but there are exceptions which make it only virtual. There are, for example, wines of extremely high quality that can only be inserted in the IGT category because, in their production areas, the grape blend or the varietals used in the wine are not included in the local DOC legislations. For example, the Tuscan wine Tignanello or the Umbrian San Giorgio: although these are formally classified as IGT wines, they are recognized as excellent quality wines, so much so that they are called in viticultural slang *Supervinodatavola* (super-table-wines) and can reach market prices that often are higher than those of DOC and DOCG wines. There are still more indications that better qualify DOC wines produced from particularly prized vineyards. One of these is the name *vigna* (vineyard) with a specification of place name or the geographic location of grape production. In French, this concept is expressed with the term *cru* indicating the vineyard as well as specific organoleptic characteristics of the wine that are closely bound to that particular territory.

The term *riserva* is attributed to wines that are aged for at least 2 years. DOC wines that also have an indication of the sub-zone or *riserva, superiore, vigna* or other traditional indications, cannot be packaged in containers other than glass bottles (such as bag-in-box), which have, on the contrary, been approved for regular DOC wines.

Table wines: the so-called common wines located at the base of the imaginary pyramid. These are qualitatively simple wines that are identified only by colour, name of the producer or brand; no other abbreviations can be put on the label.

IGT (Indicazione Geografica Tipica): typical geographic denomination represents the second level, with appellations that, in some cases, include entire regions. The "legislation" defines the varietals allowed (no obligation in the percentages of them), maximum yields per hectare and the quantity of wine that can be obtained per kilogram of grapes, minimum alcoholic strength and other chemical parameters. IGT wines can indicate on the label, in addition to the colour of the wine, the name of the varietal(s) and the production year. It is obligatory to indicate the *Indicazione Geografica Tipica* on the label. In order to be called with the name of one single varietal, the wine must contain at least 85% of that grape.

DOC (Denominazione d'Origine Controllata – Controlled Appellation of Origin): the third level, on the basis of even more restrictive criteria, are the wines produced in certain areas (usually small and medium sized) that correspond to certain chemical and organoleptic characteristics regulated by a specific production legislation. Stringent rules set out the territory of origin, the maximum yield in grapes and in wine, some of the chemical parameters that the wine must possess (alcoholic strength, acidity, dry extract, etc.) as well as refining method and times. The wines that aspire to receiving the DOC appellation must undergo a chemical-physical and organoleptic exam carried out by a special commission at the respective Chamber of Commerce before bottling. Only after that approval can they be marketed as DOC wines. The words Denominazione d'Origine Controllata and the name of the appellation and the vintage year must be indicated on the label even if the wine has its own brand name. There are about 700 DOC wines in Italy.

DOCG (Denominazione d'Origine Controllata e Garantita – Controlled and Guaranteed Appellation of Origin): the highest level. Few wines are in this category; they must have been previously included in the DOC category for at least 5 years and, due to their recognition and high commercial value, can then be deserving of this more prestigious appellation. The production legislation is even more restrictive than for DOC wines. In order to be recognized as DOCG wines, they must undergo strict analytical and organoleptic exams before bottling and can be marketed as DOCG wines only after having received the certificate of suitability from the respective Chamber of Commerce. Also in this case, the words *Denominazione d'Origine Controllata e Garantita,* the appellation name and the vintage year must be indicated on the label. DOCG wines cannot be sold in containers larger than 5 litres.

An example of a VQPRD wine is the Torgiano Rosso Riserva DOCG, since it is a premium wine at the top of the pyramid, aged for at least 3 years, produced with Sangiovese and Canaiolo grapes from the prized Monticchio Vineyard.

GLASSES

According to the different glass shapes, the scent of a wine can expand with greater or lesser ease or can remain focused. In addition, the points of the tongue (taste buds, page 55) that are reached by a wine served in particularly wide glasses (for example, balloon glasses) will be quite different from those reached by wine served in a long, narrow glass, something which glass designers are well aware of! In wine glasses, the stem has a very important function. It avoids warming the wine, as the glass is held by the stem (never by the bowl!). The glass should also be rinsed with a very small amount of wine before pouring the serving, to be certain that extraneous smells, such as detergent, do not remain in the glass and interfere with the wine.

A BIT OF HISTORY...

NOWADAYS THERE ARE MANY TYPES OF GLASSES ON THE MARKET, BUT IN ANTIQUITY THAT WAS NOT SO. THE USE OF DRINKING VESSELS MADE OF GLASS TO APPRECIATE WINE COLOUR AND BOUQUET GOES BACK TO THE TIME OF THE ANCIENT ROMANS, WHO HAD LEARNED THE ART OF GLASSMAKING FROM THE SYRIANS. THE PERSIANS AND OTHER MIDDLE EASTERN CULTURES, ON THE OTHER HAND, USED CERAMIC, GOLDEN OR SILVER CUPS, OR ON SPECIAL OCCASIONS, PARTICULARLY PRIZED GLASSES IN A HORN SHAPE.
UP TO THE MID 16TH CENTURY, TABLES WERE SET WITH ONLY ONE GLASS THAT WOULD BE USED BY EVERY-ONE OR AT THE MOST, ON THE TABLES OF THE RICH, FOR TWO OR THREE PEOPLE. THIS SHARING BROUGHT ABOUT THE RULE OF ETIQUETTE OF CLEANING ONE'S MOUTH WITH A NAPKIN BEFORE DRINKING IN A COMMON CUP. IN FRANCE, THE CUP WOULD NOT REMAIN ON THE TABLE, BUT ON THE SIDEBOARD, WHERE THE SERV-ANT WOULD PUT IT BACK, ALONG WITH THE BOTTLE, AFTER THE DINER HAD FINISHED DRINKING.
IN 1604 GIOVANNI MAGGI – A ROMAN DESIGNER, AUTHOR OF "BICHIEROGRAFIA " (THE GLASS DESIGN BOOK) DEDICATED TO CARDINAL FRANCESCO MARIA DEL MONTE – COMPOSED FOUR CODICES COLLECTING 1,600 DRAWINGS OF THE MOST UNUSUAL GLASSES AND BOTTLES OF THE CENTURY.

... AND AN ANECDOTE

IN ANCIENT ROME IT WAS CUSTOMARY TO TOAST ONE'S WOMAN BY DRINKING THE SAME NUMBER OF CUPS (KYATHOI) AS THE NUMBER OF LETTERS IN HER NAME. LATIN POET M. VALERIUS MARTIAL TELLS US: "SEVEN CUPS TO GIUSTINA, TO LEVINA YOU DRINK SIX, FIVE TO LICIA, FOUR TO LIDA, TO IDA THREE".

THE MOST COMMON SHAPES

A) Young and Fresh Whites
B) Mature, Structured Whites
C) Young and Fresh Rosés
D) Mature, Structured Rosés

GLASSES FOR WHITES AND ROSÉS

A) Young Reds
B) Medium-Bodied Reds
C) Very Mature, Structured Reds
D) Very Mature, Structured Reds

GLASSES FOR REDS

A) Sweet and Passito Wines
B) Fortified Wines

GLASSES FOR SWEET AND FORTIFIED WINES

A) "Charmat" Method
B) Classical Method and Champagne
C) Mature and Vintage Classical
   Method and Champagne
D) Sweet Aromatic Wines

GLASSES FOR SPARKLING WINES

BOTTLES: SIZES AND CAPACITIES

The standard capacity of a bottle of wine is conventionally 0.75 litres (equal to 750ml) while the half bottle (0.375 litres or 375ml) is often used for dessert wines. There are also the rare, large sizes that are generally designated by names of Biblical characters.

Bottle name	Capacity (in liters)	Equivalence in standard bottles
Mignonnette	0.03-0.05 lt (30-50 ml)	About 1/25
Quarter-bottle or split	0.20-0.187 lt (187-200 ml)	About 1/4
Half bottle (or Fillette)	Half bottle (or Fillette)	1/2
Petite bouteille (little bottle)	0.50 lt (500 ml)	2/3
Standard bottle	0.75 lt (750 ml)	1
Magnum	1.5 (1500 ml)	2
Double Magnum or Jéroboam	3 (3000 ml)	4
Réhoboam	4,5	6
Mathuselah or Imperial	6	8
Salmanazar	9	12
Balthazar	12	16
Nebuchadnezzar	15	20
Melchior or Salomon	18	24
Primat	27	36
Melchizedek	30	40

ANECDOTE

STRAW-COVERED GLASS FLASKS FIRST APPEARED TOWARDS THE END OF THE 14TH CENTURY IN TUSCANY AND SLOWLY SUBSTITUTED THE TIN-PLATED METAL CONTAINERS THEN IN USE. ONLY IN THE 1500'S DID GLASS BEGIN TO BE MORE WIDELY USED TO STORE WINE, BUT A CENTURY LATER, BY BURNING COAL FOR GLASSMAKING, THE FUSION TEMPERATURES WERE HIGH ENOUGH (1500 °C /2732 °F) THAT GLASS BOTTLES BECAME SIGNIFICANTLY RESISTANT, BOTH FOR TRANSPORTATION AND FOR DOMESTIC USE. THE FIRST GLASS WINE BOTTLE WAS PRODUCED IN 1632 BY SIR KENELM DIGBY, BUT WAS COPYRIGHTED ONLY IN 1661 BY JOHN COLNETT WHO TOOK THE CREDIT FOR IT. IT WAS A DARK GLASS BOTTLE, STRONG AND HEAVY WITH A BALL-SHAPED BODY AND NARROWING BASE. THE NECK WAS REINFORCED BY A RING PLACED A FEW CENTIMETRES BELOW THE MOUTH WHICH HELD A PAPER OR PARCHMENT CAP BY A STRING. ONLY IN THE 19TH CENTURY, HOWEVER, WHEN THE CONTAINER COST LESS THAN THE CONTENTS, DID BOTTLES BEGIN TO BE USED TO STORE WINE; PREVIOUSLY, AS IN ANCIENT TIMES, BOTTLES WERE USED AS SERVING VESSELS AND THE CONSUMER WOULD TRANSFER THE WINE FROM ANOTHER TYPE OF CONTAINER.

COMMON TYPES OF WINE BOTTLES

ALBA BOTTLE: a cone-shaped cylindrical bottle similar to the Burgundy bottle (see below); used in Piedmont for red wines like Barolo, Barbera and Dolcetto.

BORDEAUX: the most widely used both for whites (often in transparent glass) and for reds (in dark glass, either green or brown). It comes in various heights. Traditionally used in the Bordeaux region of France, it is now used worldwide. There is also a version with a "high shoulder" normally used for prestigious wines.

BURGUNDY OR **BURGUNDIAN:** typical of Burgundy in France. Suitable both for white and red wines, it is widely used all over the world. The glass is dark green or brown for reds, sometimes light green for whites.

CHAMPAGNE BOTTLE: traditionally used for Champagne and other spumante wines, it is similar to the Burgundy bottle, but has a wider and thicker base, heavier glass to withstand the internal pressure (up to 10 atmospheres). The mouth has an outer lip for fixing the wire cage, or muzzle, that holds the cork.

FLASK: a typical container of the Chianti area in Tuscany obtained by blowing glass into almost a sphere and wrapping with woven straw to keep the bottle standing and protect it from blows. Once very common, it is almost never used now because of high production costs for the straw covering, storage problems and above all because it is not compatible with the image of a quality wine.

RHENISH: also called "Alsatian", common in the Rhine area in Germany, its shape is very elongated cylindrical-conical and it is used essentially for white wines.

WHAT THEY'VE SAID
famous phrases about wine

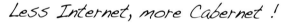

Less Internet, more Cabernet !

Anonymus (written on wall)

...look at the sun's heat that becomes wine when combined with the juice that flows from the vine...

Dante Alighieri

He who drinks only water has a secret to hide.

Charles Baudelaire

True wine lovers don't drink wine: they taste secrets.

Salvador Dalí

In vino veritas.

Plinio

Wine is the song of the earth towards the heavens.

Luigi Veronelli

INDEX OF TECHNICAL TERMS

DON'T MISS THE NEXT EPISODE: A JOURNEY
WITHIN THE MUSEUM... OF WINE

A JOURNEY ACROSS 5000 YEARS OF THE HISTORY OF GRAPES AND WINE, WHICH HAVE SO SIGNIFICANTLY INFLUENCED ECONOMICS, CIVILIZATION, ARTS AND CRAFTS. A UNIQUE MUSEUM THAT ATTRACTS VISITORS OF ALL AGES FROM ALL OVER THE WORLD.
NEARLY FOUR THOUSAND ARTEFACTS AND NUMEROUS IMPORTANT ART COLLECTIONS DISPLAYED IN A SMALL 16TH-CENTURY MANSION: IT'S CALLED THE WINE MUSEUM BUT, UNEXPECTEDLY AND SURPRISINGLY, THERE IS NOT A SINGLE BOTTLE OF WINE. IT'S NOT NEEDED, BECAUSE WINE IS EVERYWHERE: IN THE AIR, IN THE IMPRINTS OF CRAFTSMEN ON THE ANTIQUE TOOLS, IN THE THE INSPIRATION OF THE ARTISTS WHO CRE-ATED THE WORKS ON DISPLAY, FROM CERAMICS TO ENGRAVINGS; WINE IS IN THE OBJECTS AND THE ATMOSPHERE AS WELL AS THE SURROUNDING COUNTRYSIDE. IT IS EVERYWHERE BECAUSE IT IS ALSO PART OF THE COL-LECTIVE IMAGINATION. SO DON'T MISS THE NEXT JOURNEY, AMONG THE PIECES DISPLAYED THERE THAT WILL ALMOST MAGICALLY COME TO LIFE AND TELL THEIR OWN HISTORY OF WINE.